SPARKNOTES®

ACT* math & science WORKBOOK

© 2007, 2005, 2004, 2003, 2002 by Spark Publishing

Spark Publishing
A Division of Barnes & Noble
120 Fifth Avenue
New York, NY 10011
www.sparknotes.com

Please submit changes or report errors to www.sparknotes.com/errors.

ISBN 13: 978-1-4114-9676-7
ISBN 10: 1-4114-9676-0

Printed and bound in Canada.

10 9 8 7 6

CONTENTS

Overview of the ACT Science Reasoning Test 133

Review for the ACT Science Reasoning Test 139

Practice for the ACT Science Reasoning Test 159

I TRODUCTIO

Welcome to the *SparkNotes ACT Math & Science Workbook*. No doubt you've bought this book because you need some extra practice for the Math and Science Reasoning Tests. You've come to the right place. We created this workbook to give you targeted practice, as well as a thorough review of the topics covered by these two sections on the ACT.

This workbook comes equipped with specific test-taking strategies that will help you on the Math and Science Tests. After learning the test-taking strategies and drilling yourself with 137 practice questions, you should be ready to ace the Math and Science Reasoning Tests on the ACT.

Let's begin by looking at the entire ACT. This chapter will explain all the topics the ACT covers, how it's formatted and organized, and how it's scored.

CONTENT AND STRUCTURE OF THE ACT

The writers of the ACT pride themselves on the regularity and predictability of their tests. They claim that every test has the same breakdown of question types. For example, every English Test contains ten punctuation questions, and every Math Test contains four trigonometry questions. The ACT writers believe that it is very important to maintain these numbers exactly. The numbers of questions will not vary.

The essential unchanging content of the ACT means you can be thoroughly prepared for the test. The ACT writers don't want to trick you. They want to tell you exactly what will be on the test and give you every chance in the world to prepare for it. The exam will test your knowledge, and it makes sense that the best way to do that is to let you know precisely what you need to know and then see how well you can learn it. You won't be caught off guard by unfamiliar material on test day. Phew!

The ACT consists of four multiple-choice tests covering English, Math, Reading, and Science Reasoning. The optional writing section is tacked on to the very end of the test. These subject tests will always appear on the ACT in the order in which we just named them. The following provides a brief summary of the four sections and optional Writing Test:

- **The English Test (75 Questions, 45 Minutes).** The English Test contains five reading passages containing grammatical and stylistic errors. Each passage is accompanied by fifteen questions. You are given 45 minutes to answer these 75 questions, which will test your ability to make corrections. The English Test assesses your understanding of basic grammar, as well as your grasp of the tools and strategies a writer can use to put sentences together to form paragraphs and arguments.

- **The Math Test (60 Questions, 60 Minutes).** The Math Test covers six areas of high school math: pre-algebra, elementary algebra, intermediate algebra, coordinate geometry, plane geometry, and trigonometry. The majority of questions deal with pre-algebra, elementary algebra, and plane geometry, which are topics usually covered at the beginning of high school. The other three topics—intermediate algebra, coordinate geometry, and trigonometry—constitute only 22 of the 60 questions on the test. You should learn these more difficult topics by the end of your junior year in high school. If you have not learned trigonometry by that time, don't sweat it: There are only four trig questions on the test, and four questions won't ruin your score. The Math Test differs from the other tests in two significant ways:

1. You're allowed to use a calculator.
2. There are five answer choices for each question, rather than four.

Later in the guide, we'll discuss how these differences should affect your strategy on the Math Test.

- **The Reading Test (40 Questions, 35 Minutes).** The Reading Test consists of four passages, each approximately 750 words long. The passages cover prose fiction, social science, humanities, and natural science. These passages always appear in the above order, and they are given equal weight in scoring. Each passage is accompanied by ten questions of varying levels of difficulty. Unlike the English and Math Tests, the Reading Test evaluates a set of skills you've acquired, rather than your mastery of subjects you've learned. As the name of this test implies, these skills are your ability to read and to comprehend different types of passages.

- **The Science Reasoning Test (40 Questions, 35 Minutes).** Despite its intimidating name, Science Reasoning doesn't test your understanding of any scientific field. Instead, this test assesses your ability to "reason like a scientist" or to understand and analyze data. All of the information you need to know for the Science Reasoning Test will be presented in the questions. You just have to dig it out. The Science Reasoning Test consists of seven passages that contain a mixture of graphs, charts, and explanatory text. Each passage is followed by five to seven questions.

- **The Writing Test (1 Essay Question, 30 Minutes).** The Writing Test, which comes at the end of the exam, gives you 30 minutes to construct an essay based on a certain issue. The issue will be relevant to your life as a high school student. You can either choose to support the perspective given on the issue or provide one from your own experience.

ACT SCORING AND THE SCORE REPORT

The way the ACT is scored might be the most confusing aspect of the test. The number of scores a single ACT test produces is mind-boggling.

- First, you receive **four raw scores,** one for each subject test, in addition to **raw subscores** for subsections of the subject test (for example, Pre-Algebra/Elementary Algebra, Intermediate Algebra/Coordinate Geometry, and Plane Geometry/Trigonometry are the three subsections of the Math Test).
- Those raw scores are converted into **four scaled scores** for the subject tests and **scaled subscores** for the subsections.
- The four scaled scores are averaged, producing the **Composite Score.**
- Finally, every single score is assigned a corresponding **percentile ranking,** indicating how you fared in comparison to other test-takers.

The two scores that will matter most to you and to colleges are the Composite Score and the overall percentile ranking. You will receive these two numbers, plus your scaled scores and subscores, in a score report about four to seven weeks after you take the test.

Raw Scores

Although you will never see a raw score on your score report, you should know how the raw score is computed. All raw scores are based on the number of questions you answered correctly. To compute the raw score of a subject test, simply count up the number of questions you answered correctly in that subject test. For each correct answer, you receive one point. Your raw score is the total number of points you receive. There are no point deductions for wrong answers.

Raw Subscores

Each subject test contains component subsections, each of which is assigned a raw subscore. For example, the Math Test breaks down into Pre-Algebra/Elementary Algebra, Intermediate Algebra/Coordinate Geometry, and Plane Geometry/Trigonometry. Let's say you correctly answered 23 Pre-Algebra/Elementary Algebra questions, 17 Intermediate Algebra/Coordinate Geometry questions, and 6 Plane Geometry/Trigonometry questions on the Math Test. Your raw score for those three subsections would be 23, 17, and 6, respectively.

Scoring Practice Sets

This workbook is geared toward helping you find your strengths and weaknesses by taking the math and science practice sets. Use the practice sets to figure out in which areas you need a little more help, then focus your study time on those. For example, if you find yourself answering more Algebra questions correctly than Trigonometry, you should devote more time to brushing up on Trigonometry in the review section.

ACT Scores and the Optional Writing Test

The Writing Test is graded on a scale of 1 to 6. Two raters will grade your essay, and their scores will be added for a final subscore between 2–12. This subscore will then be combined with the English score to create a "Combined English/Writing score," on a 1–36 scale. This score, along with the Writing Test subscore, is listed on your score report in addition to the regular battery of scores. Also, the Writing Test answer sheet will be scanned and made available for download, so institutions will be able to read exactly what you wrote.

SPECIAL NOTE: If you take the Writing Test, all scores, including the Combined English/Writing score and Writing subscore, will be sent to all the institutions you requested to receive your scores during the registration process. *This is regardless of whether or not those schools require the Writing Test.* A school must specifically request not to receive the results of the Writing Test or they will be sent to the school automatically.

Percentile Rankings

Percentile rankings indicate how you performed compared to the other students in the nation who took the same test you did. A percentile ranking of 75 means that 74 percent of test-takers scored worse than you and 25 percent scored the same or better.

The percentile rankings that matter most are the ones given for each subject test and the one accompanying the Composite Score (the following chart gives a sampling of percentile rankings and their corresponding Composite Scores). You will receive these percentiles on your score report.

The Composite Score

The Composite Score is the big one. It is the score your parents will tell their friends and the one your curious peers will want to know. More precisely, it is the average of your scaled scores for the four tests. So, if you got a 28 on the English Test, a 26 on the Math Test, a 32 on the Reading Test, and a 30 on the Science Reasoning Test, your composite score will be:

$$\frac{28+26+32+30}{4} = \frac{116}{4} = 29$$

On your score report, look for the Composite Score at the bottom of the page.

Correspondence of Composite Score, Percentile Rank & Correct Answers

The chart below shows a sample of Composite Scores and how they correspond to percentile rankings and percentages of questions answered correctly. This chart should give you some context for understanding the relative levels of achievement indicated by these Composite Scores:

Composite Score	ACT Approximate Percentile Rank	Approximate Percentage of Correct Answers
31	98%	89%
26	86%	76%
23	70%	66%
20	49%	55%
17	26%	44%

Who Receives the Scores? Not You.

That heading is a little misleading, but we thought we'd draw your attention to a bizarre aspect of the test. If you follow the ACT's registration instructions, you probably *won't* receive your score directly—your high school guidance counselor and any colleges you list (see "Sending Scores to Colleges") will get it first, and then you must retrieve your score from your guidance counselor. But there are ways around this bureaucracy.

If you want to receive the report directly at home rather than through a third party at your high school, you can do one of two things:

1. Have your high school give the ACT test company permission to send your score to your home.
2. Leave the High School Code blank when you sign up for the test.

Option 2 is less complicated than Option 1, and there are no repercussions from leaving the Code blank. Although ACT won't explicitly tell you about Option 2, it will work.

Early Score by Web

Now you are able to view your ACT score report ten to fifteen days after you take the test, and well before the four to seven weeks it normally takes them to mail the scores to you. Simply log on to **actstudent.org** and locate Early Scores by Web. Of course there is a cost involved, as with most things related to the ACT, and satisfying your need to know will cost you $8. Note that it is $8 each time you view your scores, not a flat $8 fee, so make sure you print that score report page the first time you view it. Also, this feature is only available for national test dates.

Sending Scores to Colleges

In the moments before you take the ACT, the test administrators will give you a form allowing you to submit a list of up to six colleges that will receive your score directly from the company that makes the test. Don't submit a list unless you feel extremely confident that you will achieve your target score on the exam. After all, once you receive your score report and *know* you got the score you wanted, you can always order score reports to be sent to colleges. True, forwarding your scores costs a small fee after the first three reports, but the security it provides is worth it.

There is only one reason why you should opt to have your score sent directly to colleges. If you take the test near college application deadlines, you will probably have to choose this service to ensure that your scores arrive at the colleges on time.

Canceling the Score Report

If you choose to send your score report directly to colleges, but then have a really horrible day at the test center, don't panic. You have several days to cancel your score report. To do this, call ACT at (319) 337-1270. You have until noon, Central Standard Time, on the Thursday immediately following your test date to cancel your score.

Taking the ACT Twice (or Three Times)

If you have a really horrible day at the test center but you *didn't* choose to send your score report directly to colleges, don't cancel the report. No matter how many times you take the ACT, the colleges you apply to will see only one of your scores—the one you pick. If you don't score as well as you want to the first time, you can take the test again (and again and again) with impunity until you receive a score with which you are happy.

You have a good opportunity to improve your ACT score on the second try. More than half of second-time test-takers increase their scores. Taking the test a third or a fourth time probably won't make much difference in your score unless something went seriously awry on your previous tries.

WHAT AN ACT SCORE MEANS

You've taken the test and received your score; now what happens? If you're still in your junior year of high school, your ACT score can help you determine which colleges to apply to. Numerous publications each year publish reports on college profiles. Both these reports and your high school guidance counselor should help you determine your safety, 50/50, and reach schools, based on your ACT score, high school GPA, and other factors such as recommendations and extracurricular activities. While an applicant's total package is what counts, a good ACT score will never hurt your chances of getting into the schools you want. If you scored better than you expected, your score may help your applications at schools that you previously considered reaches.

How Your ACT Score Fits into Your Application Package

You may be wondering why a standardized test score matters in your college application. Let's compare two students, Megan and Chloe. Megan and Chloe are straight-A students at their respective high schools. These grades reflect the girls' relative standings at their schools (unless everyone at these two schools gets As), but how can college administrator Tim use these grades to compare Megan and Chloe? It seems like we're leading you to answer,

"ACT scores!" Well, that's not entirely true. The truth is that Tim will look at a number of things to differentiate between the two girls. He'll carefully consider extracurricular activities, the girls' essays, and their recommendations. He'll also look at course descriptions to see whether Megan has long been acing Advanced Number Theory and Sanskrit while Chloe has been queen of her shop class.

So where does the ACT fit into this? Well, it's just another way of confirming relative standing among applicants. Tim may have access to course descriptions, but that curious college administrator is always on the lookout for other means of comparison. The ACT provides that means: It is a national standard by which colleges can evaluate applicants.

The ACT is merely one factor in your total application package, but it is an important factor that should not be overlooked or slighted. Although many schools hesitate to admit it, the fact is that your ACT score is one of the first things that stands out to someone reading your application. That person will eventually get around to reading teacher recommendations and your personal essay, but your ACT score is an easily digestible piece of information that will allow an admissions staff to form an early impression of your academic achievement. We're telling you this not to scare you, but to give you an honest assessment of what the ACT means to your college application.

That said, you should think of the ACT not as an adversary but as a tool that will help you get into college. For example, if Chloe is really a class-A student, but her high school doesn't give her the opportunity to extend her talents beyond shop class, the ACT provides an opportunity for her to show Tim she isn't a flake. If you approach the ACT pragmatically and don't hope for a knockout score you can't achieve, and if you study with some vigor, you can control your ACT destiny and get the score you need in order to get into the colleges of your choice.

WHEN TO TAKE THE TEST

Most people take the ACT at the end of junior year or the beginning of senior year. We recommend taking it at the end of junior year for a number of reasons:

1. Taking the test junior year will give you time to retake it if necessary.
2. You will have covered most of the material on the ACT by the end of junior year, and it will be fresh in your mind.
3. You are likely to forget some material during the summer before your senior year.

Ultimately, when you choose to take the test depends on only one thing: you. If you don't feel comfortable taking it junior year, spend some time during the summer reviewing and take the test during the fall of your senior year. If you are applying for regular admission to colleges, you will probably have a couple of test dates to choose from during your senior year, but take the earliest possible test if you are applying for early admission.

ACT Registration

To register for the ACT, you must first obtain an ACT registration packet. Your high school guidance counselor will probably have these packets available for you. If you can't get the packet through your high school, you can write or call ACT at:

> ACT Registration
> P.O. Box 414
> Iowa City, IA 52243-0414
> (319) 337-1270

You can also register for the test by visiting ACT's student website (**actstudent.org**) or, if your high school has it, by using ACT's software program College Connector. If you have taken the ACT within the last two years, you may reregister over the phone for an additional fee. You must make a VISA or MasterCard payment if you register on the Web, through College Connector, or by phone.

Regular, Late, and Standby Registration

There are three types of registration: regular, late, and standby.

- Regular registration deadlines are approximately five weeks before the test date. The basic fee is $29 in the U.S. and $49 for students testing internationally. In addition to the basic fee, the optional Writing Test is $14 for all students.
- Late registration, which costs you an additional $19, ends three weeks before the test date.

The ACT registration packet will contain the exact dates for regular and late registration deadlines.

- Standby registration is for those students who missed the late registration deadline and need to take the test by a certain date. Standby registration occurs on the day of the test. It costs an additional $39, and it does not guarantee you a seat or a test booklet. Standby registration is a last resort. If you must use standby registration, make sure to bring a completed registration folder, fee payment, and appropriate personal identification to the test center.

The ACT Admission Ticket

If you have registered for the ACT using regular or late registration, you will receive an admission ticket in the mail. This ticket will tell you when and where the test will be administered. It will also list the information you submitted to ACT, such as any colleges that will receive your score directly. You should read the admission ticket carefully to make sure there are no mistakes. If you find a mistake, follow the instructions on the back of the ticket for correcting information.

Test Dates

ACT test dates usually fall in October, December, February, April, and June. Certain states also have a September test date. Double-check your test dates by going to ACT's student website at **actstudent.org**.

GENErAL TEST-TAKI G STRATEGIES

In this section, you'll learn how to take advantage of the ACT's structure to achieve the score you want. You'll learn basic rules for taking the ACT, as well as pacing and preparation strategies. These are the general test-taking strategies that you should use in all sections of the test, not just the Math and Science Reasoning Tests. There are, of course, specific strategies for each of the individual tests. We'll cover the specific strategies for Math and Science Reasoning in this workbook.

SEVEN BASIC RULES FOR TAKING THE ACT

These seven rules apply to every section of the ACT. We list them here because you should always have these rules of test-taking resting gently in your mind as you take the test. You don't need to focus on them obsessively, but you should be sure not to forget them. They will help you save time and cut down on careless errors.

1. **Know the instructions for each test.** Since you'll need all the time you can get, don't waste time reading the test instructions during the actual test. Read the instructions before taking each practice set so you'll have them memorized for the actual test.

2. **Use your test booklet as scratch paper.** Some students seem to think their test booklet has to look "pretty" at the end of the test. Don't be one of those students. A pristine test booklet is a sad test booklet. In the Math Test, the ACT writers even give you "figuring" space for drawing diagrams and writing out solutions. You should write down all your work for math problems, in case you want to return to them later to complete the question or check your answer. The Math Test isn't the only place where you can benefit from marginal scribbling, though. Making margin notes alongside the Reading and Science Reasoning passages can help you stay on track when answering the subsequent questions. In addition, if you want to skip a question and come back to it later, you should make a distinctive mark next to it, so you won't miss it on your second pass through the questions.

3. **Answer the easy questions first.** This is a crucial strategy for the ACT. Since all questions within a subject test are worth the same number of points, there's no point in slaving away over a difficult question if doing so requires several minutes. In the same amount of time, you probably could have racked up points by answering a bunch of easy, less time-consuming questions.

    So, answer the easy and moderate questions first. That way you'll make sure that you get to see all the questions on the test that you have a good shot of getting right, while saving the leftover time for the difficult questions.

4. **Don't get bogged down by a hard question.** This rule may seem obvious, but many people have a hard time letting go of a question. If you've spent a significant amount of time on a problem (in ACT world, a minute and a half is a lot of

time) and haven't gotten close to answering it, just let it go. Leaving a question unfinished may seem like giving up or wasting time you've already spent, but you can come back to the problem after you've answered the easy ones. The time you spent on the problem earlier won't be wasted. When you come back to the problem, you'll already have done part of the work needed to solve it.

This strategy goes hand in hand with Rule 3. After all, the tough question that's chewing up your time isn't worth more to the computer grading your answer sheet than the easy questions nearby.

5. **Avoid carelessness.** There are two kinds of carelessness that threaten you as an ACT test-taker. The first kind is obvious: making mistakes because you are moving too quickly through the questions. Speeding through the test can result in misinterpreting a question or missing a crucial piece of information. You should always be aware of this kind of error because the ACT writers have written the test with speedy test-takers in mind: They often include tempting "partial answers" among the answer choices. A partial answer is the result of some, but not all, of the steps needed to solve a problem. If you rush through a question, you may mistake a partial answer for the real answer. Students often fall into the speeding trap when they become confused, since confusion brings nervousness and fear of falling behind. But those moments of confusion are precisely the moments when you should take a second to slow down. Take a deep breath, look at the question, and make a sober decision about whether or not you can answer it. If you can, dive back in. If you can't, skip the question and go on to the next one.

The second kind of carelessness arises from frustration or lack of confidence. Don't allow yourself to assume a defeatist attitude toward questions that appear to be complex. While some of these questions may actually be complex, some of them will be fairly simple questions disguised in complex-sounding terms. You should at least skim every question to see whether you have a feasible chance of answering it. Assuming you can't answer a question is like returning a present you've never even opened.

6. **Be careful bubbling in your answers.** Imagine this: You get all the right answers to the ACT questions, but you fill in all the wrong bubbles. The scoring computer doesn't care that you did the right work; all it cares about are the blackened bubbles on the answer sheet and the wrong answers that they indicate.

Protect yourself against this terrifying possibility with careful bubbling. An easy way to prevent slips on the ACT answer sheet is to pay attention to the letters being bubbled. Odd-numbered answers are lettered **A, B, C, D** (except on the Math Test, where they are **A, B, C, D, E**), and even-numbered answers are lettered **F, G, H, J** (except on the Math Test, where they are **F, G, H, J, K**).

You may also want to try bubbling in groups (five at a time or a page at a time) rather than answering one by one. Circle the answers in the test booklet as you go through the page, and then transfer the answers over to the answer sheet as a group. This method should increase your speed and accuracy in filling out the answer sheet. To further increase your accuracy, say the question number and the answer in your head as you fill out the grid: "Number 24, **F**. Number 25, **C**. Number 26, **J**."

7. **Always guess when you don't know the answer.** We will discuss guessing in the following section, "Understand 'Multiple Choice,'" but the basic rule is: always guess! You're much better off guessing than leaving an answer blank because there is no penalty for wrong answers.

UNDERSTAND "MULTIPLE CHOICE"

As we've suggested throughout this chapter, the multiple-choice format of the ACT should affect the way you approach the questions. In this section, we'll discuss exactly how.

Only the Answer Matters

A computer, not a person, will score your test. This computer does not care how you came to your answers; it cares only whether your answers are correct and readable in little oval form. The test booklet in which you worked out your answers gets thrown in the garbage, or, if your proctor is conscientious, into a recycling bin.

On the ACT, no one looks at your work. If you get a question right, it doesn't matter whether you did impeccable work. In fact, it doesn't even matter whether you knew the answer or guessed. The multiple-choice structure of the test is a message to you from the ACT: "We only care about your answers." Remember, the ACT is your tool to get into college, so treat it as a tool. It wants right answers? Give it right answers, as many as possible, using whatever strategies you can.

The Answers Are Right There

When you look at any ACT multiple-choice question, the answer is already right there in front of you. Of course, the ACT writers don't just *give* you the correct answer; they hide it among a bunch of incorrect answer choices. Your job on each question is to find the right answer. Because the answer is right there, begging to be found, you have two methods you can use to try to get the correct answer:

1. Look through the answer choices and pick out the one that is correct.
2. Look at the answer choices and eliminate wrong answers until there's only one answer left.

Both methods have their advantages: You are better off using one in some situations and the other in others. In a perfect scenario in which you are sure how to answer a question, finding the right answer immediately is clearly better than chipping away at the wrong answers. Coming to a conclusion about a problem and then picking the single correct choice is a much simpler and quicker process than going through every answer choice and discarding the four that are wrong.

However, when you are unsure how to solve the problem, eliminating wrong answers becomes more attractive and appropriate. By focusing on the answers to problems that are giving you trouble, you might be able to use the answer choices to lead you in the right direction or to solve the problem through trial and error. You also might be able to eliminate answer choices through a variety of strategies (these strategies vary, as you'll see in the chapters devoted to question types). In some cases, you might be able to eliminate all the wrong answers. In others, you might be able to eliminate only one, which will still improve your odds when you attempt to guess.

Part of your preparation for the ACT should be to get some sense of when to use each strategy. Using the right strategy can increase your speed without affecting your accuracy, giving you more time to work on and answer as many questions as possible.

Guessing

We've said it once, but it's important enough to bear repetition: Whenever you can't answer a question on the ACT, you must guess. You are not penalized for getting a question wrong, so guessing can only help your score.

Random Guessing and Educated Guessing

There are actually two kinds of guesses: random and educated. Random guesser Charlie Franklin will always guess **C** or **F** because he really, really likes those letters. Using this method, Charlie has a pretty good chance of getting about 25 percent of the questions right, yielding a Composite Score of about 11. That's not too shabby, considering Charlie expended practically no intellectual energy beyond identifying **C** and **F** as the first letters of his first and last names.

But what about educated guesser Celia? Instead of immediately guessing on each question, she works to eliminate answers, always getting rid of two choices for each question. She then guesses between the remaining choices and has a 50 percent chance of getting the correct answer. Celia will therefore get about half of the questions on the test correct. Her Composite Score will be about a 19, which is an average score on the ACT.

The example of these two guessers should show you that while blind guessing can help you, educated guessing can *really* help you. For example, let's say you know the correct answer for half of the questions and you guess randomly on the remaining half. Your score will probably be a 22—three points higher than the score you'd get leaving half of the answers blank. Now let's say you know the correct answer for half of the questions and you make educated guesses on the remaining half, narrowing the choices to two. You can probably score a 26 with this method, landing you in the 90th percentile of test-takers. This is a good score, and to get it you need to be certain of only half the answers.

"Always guess" really means "always eliminate as many answer choices as possible and then guess." Practice guessing when you take the practice sets.

A Note to the Timid Guesser

Some students feel that guessing is like cheating. They believe that by guessing, they are getting points they don't really deserve. Such a belief might be noble, but it is also mistaken, for two reasons.

First, educated guessing is actually a form of partial credit on the ACT. Let's say you're taking the ACT and come upon a question you can't quite figure out. Yet while you aren't sure of the definite answer, you are sure that two of the answer choices *can't* be right. In other words, you can eliminate two of the four answer choices, leaving you with a one in two chance of guessing correctly between the remaining two answer choices. Now let's say someone else is taking the same test and gets to the same question. But this person is completely flummoxed. He can't eliminate *any* answer choices. When this person guesses, he has only a one in four chance of guessing correctly. Your extra knowledge, which allowed you to eliminate some answer choices, gives you better odds of getting this question right, exactly as extra knowledge should.

Second, the people who made the ACT thought very hard about how the scoring of the test should work. When they decided that they wouldn't include a penalty for wrong answers, they knew that the lack of a penalty would allow people to guess. In other words, they built the test with the specific understanding that people would guess on every question they couldn't answer. The test creators *planned* for you to guess. So go ahead and do it.

PACE YOURSELF

The ACT presents you with a ton of questions and, despite its three-hour length, not that much time to answer them. As you take the test, you will probably feel some pressure to answer quickly. As we've already discussed, getting bogged down on a single question is not a good thing. But rushing isn't any good either. In the end, there's no real difference between answering very few questions and answering lots of questions incorrectly: Both will lead to low scores. What you have to do is find a happy medium, a groove, a speed at which you can be both accurate and efficient, and get the score you want. Finding this pace is a tricky task, but it will come through practice and strategy.

Keep an Eye on the Clock

Because the ACT is a timed test, you should always be aware of the time. The proctor at the test center will strictly enforce the time limits for each subject test. Even if you have only one question left to answer, you won't be allowed to fill in that bubble.

As you take the test, watch the clock. You shouldn't be checking it every two minutes, since you will only waste time and give yourself a headache. But you should check occasionally to make sure you are on pace to achieve your target score.

SET A TARGET SCORE

The ACT is your tool to get into college. Therefore, a perfect score on the ACT is not a 36; it's the score that gets you into the colleges of your choice. Once you set a target score, your efforts should be directed toward achieving *that* score and not necessarily a 36.

In setting a target score, the first rule is to be honest and realistic. Base your target score on the schools you want to attend, and use the results from your practice tests to decide what's realistic. If you score a 20 on your first practice test, your target score probably should not be a 30. Instead, aim for a 23 or 24. Your scores will likely increase on your second test simply because you'll be more experienced than you were the first time, and then you can work on getting several extra problems right on each subject test. Adjust your pacing to the score you want, but also be honest with yourself about what pace you can maintain.

PREPARE

Preparation is the key to success on the ACT. When the ACT is lurking sometime far in the future, it can be difficult to motivate yourself to study. Establishing an organized study routine can help keep you on track as you approach the test date.

Setting Up a Study Schedule

Rather than simply telling yourself to study each week, you might want to write down an actual schedule, just as you have a schedule of classes at school. Keep this schedule where you'll see it every day, and consider showing it to a parent who will nag you incessantly when you don't follow it. (You might as well use your parents' nagging capabilities to your own advantage for once.) You should reward yourself for keeping to your schedule.

You should allot at least a few hours a week to studying, depending on how much time you have before the test date. If you start preparing six weeks in advance, you might consider studying one subject per week, with the last week left over for light review. Our chapters on the Math and Science Reasoning Tests will give you a solid review of the material you need to know.

To complement your studying, take the practice sets in the weeks leading up to the test. If you're preparing for Math one week, take the Math practice sets to help focus your studying.

Test Day

You must bring the following items to the test center on the day of the test:

1. Your admission ticket.
2. Photo ID or a letter of identification.

Unless a test proctor recognizes you, you will not be allowed in the test room without appropriate identification. We also suggest that you bring the following:

3. Number Two pencils.
4. A calculator. You should bring the calculator you normally use (preferably with an extra battery). You don't want to get stuck searching frantically for the right buttons on an unfamiliar calculator.
5. A watch. Your test room may not have a clock, or the clock may not be visible from where you're sitting. Since the test proctors only call out the time five minutes before the end of each section, you have to rely on yourself to know how much time remains.
6. A snack, to keep up that energy.
7. Lucky clothes. Why not?

GET ONLINE

Last but not least, don't forget to visit us online. Go to testprep.sparknotes.com for free access to additional practice tests. Our powerful test software will pinpoint your problem areas and help you overcome your weaknesses. Based on your practice test, we will build you a personalized study plan that links to the ACT topics you need to review. We recommend that you take a practice test after you've finished the practice sets in this book. Also, take advantage of the message boards, test-taking strategies, and other test prep resources.

OVERVIEW OF THE ACT MATH TEST

The good news is the Math Test gives you more time for each question than the other subject tests. The not-so-good news is at an average of one minute per question, the Math Test is relatively difficult for most people.

However, the Math Test covers the material taught in your middle school and high school math classes. Although those classes covered a lot of ground, these are topics that you likely have a pretty good grasp on. And this workbook will provide you with a solid review of all the math fundamentals you'll need to succeed on the ACT.

THE INSTRUCTIONS

Memorize the instructions for the Math Test *before* you arrive at the test center. These instructions are long, and you should not waste a second even glancing in their direction on test day. So here they are—get to know them:

DIRECTIONS: After solving each problem, pick the correct answer from the five given and fill in the corresponding oval on your answer sheet. Solve as many problems as you can in the time allowed. Do not worry over problems that take too much time; skip them if necessary and return to them if you have time.

Calculator use is permitted on the test. Calculators can be used for any problem on the test, though calculators may be more harm than help for some questions.

Note: unless otherwise stated on the test, you should assume that:

1. Figures accompanying questions are not drawn to scale.
2. Geometric figures exist in a plane.
3. When given in a question, "line" refers to a straight line.
4. When given in a question, "average" refers to the arithmetic mean.

FORMAT OF THE MATH TEST

The format of the ACT Math Test is straightforward. ACT simply lumps all the problems into one big list of math questions. The only visible quirk in formatting is that all the questions are printed on the left half of the page, while the right half is reserved for "your figuring." We'll discuss this empty space and what you should do with it in the "Strategies" section of this chapter. There are two other aspects of Math Test questions that you should keep in mind. We'll describe them to you on the next page:

Five, Not Four, Multiple Choice Answers

Unlike the three other ACT tests, the Math Test offers you five, not four, multiple-choice answers. You should be aware of this fact when filling in the bubbles on the answer sheet. If you are answering **D** or **J**, don't automatically fill in the last bubble in the row because you'll really be filling in **E** or **K**. Again, this is just another reason to verbalize to yourself which blank you want to be filling in as you actually fill it in.

The additional answer choice will also affect your chances of guessing the right answer. If you plan to guess blindly on a math problem, your odds of getting the correct answer are one in five, or 20 percent. On the other subject tests, your chances are higher: one in four, or 25 percent. This difference of 5 percent really isn't that big of a deal and shouldn't change your guessing strategy. You should still guess on any question you can't answer. Guess blindly if you have no clue about how to answer the question. But your best bet is always to eliminate whatever answer choices you can and then guess.

Question Types

There are two kinds of questions on the ACT Math Test: basic problems and word problems. Word problems tend to be more difficult than basic problems simply because they require the additional step of translating the words into a numerical problem that you can solve. Of course, a basic problem on a complex topic will still likely be more difficult than a word problem on a very easy topic.

Basic Problems

Basic math problems are exactly how they sound: basic. You won't see any complicated wording or context in these problems. They simply present you with a math problem in a no-frills fashion. If you encounter a basic math problem that asks you to calculate what two plus two is (you won't), the question would look like this:

$$2 + 2 = ?$$

That's pretty straightforward; you shouldn't have a problem figuring out what this question wants you to do.

Word Problems

Word problems are so named because they use words to describe a math problem. These questions are by nature more complicated than basic math problems because you have to sort through the words to figure out the math problem beneath them. In essence, you have two steps: figuring out what the math problem is and then solving it.

For example, if you were asked for the same calculation of two plus two as a word problem, it might look something like this:

Allison has 2 green apples, and Jen has 2 red apples. Together, how many apples do Allison and Jen have?

This question isn't exactly complicated, but it is certainly more complicated than the basic version of the problem. The setting of the problem, rather than elucidating the question, only adds to its complexity. Your job on this and all word problems is to sort through the muck and translate the words into a straightforward math problem. A question like "Together, how many apples do Allison and Jen have?" really means "Allison's apples plus Jen's apples equals what?", or, ultimately, "Two plus two equals what?"

CONTENT OF THE MATH TEST

The ACT Math Test covers a broad array of topics, from simple topics like pre-algebra to more difficult ones such as trigonometry. You shouldn't assume that the pre-algebra questions will be a thousand times easier than the trig questions, though. To compensate for their relative difficulty, ACT usually uses the basic format to ask you questions on trig. Pre-algebra questions, on the other hand, run the gamut of difficulty, so don't slight them in your math review.

Below we list the general topics that are covered on the Math Test:

- **Pre-Algebra:** number problems; multiples, factors, and primes; divisibility and remainders; percentages; ratios and proportions; mean, median, and mode; probability; absolute value; exponents and roots; series
- **Elementary Algebra:** substitution, simplifying algebraic expressions, writing expressions and equations, solving linear equations, multiplying binomials, inequalities
- **Intermediate Algebra:** solving and factoring quadratic equations, solving systems of equations, relationship between sides of an equation, functions, matrices
- **Coordinate Geometry:** number lines and inequalities, the (x, y) coordinate plane, distance and midpoints, slope, parallel and perpendicular lines, graphing equations, conic sections
- **Plane Geometry:** angles, triangles, polygons, circles, simple 3-D geometry
- **Trigonometry:** SOHCAHTOA, solving triangles, trigonometric identities, trigonometric graphs

As part of our ACT Math review, we will tell you which topics appear often and which pop up only occasionally, and we'll give you practice in each specific math area. Make sure you read our math strategies in the next section.

STRATEGIES FOR THE MATH TEST

The most important strategy for doing well on the Math Test is to give yourself a good deal of time to review math. In this section, we will help you to approach the Math Test, but you should not think of the strategies and methods we provide as substitutions for knowledge of math. They are meant to augment your understanding of math. Good strategies can help you put your knowledge of math and the ACT format to the best possible use. They can't replace knowledge of math.

Even if you're dominating your math class this year, you'll benefit from a full review because the material covered on this test is quite broad and can reach back to the math you studied in seventh grade. Those subjects aren't hard, but they may cover minor details that you've forgotten—and which could be important on the test.

With that gentle warning in mind, you can peruse the following strategies section for really helpful tips for taking the test. Reading and understanding these tips alone isn't going to get you a perfect score on the test, but applying them along with your math skills will definitely help you achieve your target score.

Use Your Calculator Wisely

Just because calculator use is permitted on the Math Test doesn't mean you should go calculator crazy. Calculators can certainly be helpful on some problems, but on others using a calculator might actually take more time than working the problem out by hand.

Sometimes the ACT will hint that you should stay away from the calculator. You can find this hint in the answer choices. If a fraction problem gives all the answers in fraction, not decimal, form, you should not use your calculator. You'll only be wasting time converting your decimal answer to fraction form. This rule also applies to problems involving radicals or any other answer where the answer is not worked out to some final number. There's no reason ever to touch a calculator when you're dealing with variables.

When you use your calculator on the test, it should be because you've thought about the question, you have a good sense of how to proceed, and you see how your calculator can help you. You should use your calculator only when you have a definite operation you want to perform. You should not reach for your calculator instinctively any time you run into trouble.

Questions on the ACT are designed to be answered within a minute, if that. They do not involve intense calculation. If you find yourself reaching for a calculator to work out $\sqrt{934}$, you can be certain that you've made a mistake somewhere. No calculation on the test should be that difficult.

Use Your Same Old Calculator (and Make Sure the Battery Is New)

Don't purchase a fancy calculator with 500 buttons and 600 functions for the ACT. If that's the kind of calculator you always use and you feel comfortable using it, then go ahead and bring it to the test. But if you use the basic standby, you should bring that to the test.

The ACT test center is not the place to break in a new calculator, particularly if it's one with a lot of buttons. By the time you've figured out how to turn the stupid thing on and find all the buttons, the Math Test will be over.

Now imagine for a moment that we are a nosy parent. Make sure your battery is new! This advice may seem anal, but do you really want to be the person whose battery fails halfway through the test?

Encourage Your Inner Artist

The ACT wants to bring out the artist in you, and we think they've got the right idea. On the right-hand side of every Math Test page, you will find a column with the header "DO YOUR FIGURING HERE." You can use this space to write formulas, graphs, drawings of triangles, or whatever else you want.

This space can be particularly useful for drawing figures that are not provided with the question. If you have a hard time visualizing shapes in your head, you can draw them in the figuring space. If a question asks you about angles in a polygon but doesn't provide a figure, you can make your own if it helps you solve the problem.

While writing out your answers can be extremely helpful, it can also be time consuming. Be careful not to write out all your work, if some of that work is merely aesthetic. Remember, no one will see your test booklet, and only the bubble answers count. Don't bother being neat or thorough in this scribble space. You should not do work as if you're trying to impress your teacher. You should do just as much work as you need to do in order to get the question right: no more, no less.

Avoid Partial Answers

For problems that have more than one step, a partial answer is the answer to one of the steps of the problem, but not to the whole problem. For example:

On Monday, a bus carries 10 girls and 5 boys. On Tuesday, it carries 5 girls and 6 boys. What is the average number of girls and boys on the bus over the period of Monday and Tuesday?

A. 0
B. 11
C. 13
D. 15
E. 26

The correct answer to this question is **C**, 13 girls and boys, but you may have liked **B**, **D**, or **E**, which are all partial answers to this problem (A is just silly). Here's why you might have chosen **B**, **D**, or **E**: **B** is the total number of passengers on the Tuesday bus; **D** is the total number of passengers on the Monday bus; **E** is the total number of passengers riding for both days. You have to calculate each one of these numbers to get the final answer (**E** divided by the number of days, 2). At any point during those calculations, you may have looked down and seen that a number you had calculated matched a number in the answer choices. Then you may have assumed you found the right answer. But, no, you didn't.

Partial answers love to prey upon eager test-takers who are in a hurry to get the right answer. Instead of paying careful attention to the question, these test-takers get a number, see it in the answer choices, and immediately identify it as the correct answer. The test-writers know about all these eager, jumpy test-takers and deliberately plant partial answers throughout the Math Test.

On word problems, the last sentence of the problem usually tells you what the question is looking for. Consider rereading this last sentence once you've formulated your answer to make sure you did what the question asked.

Understand "Order of Difficulty"

Knowing the order of difficulty will help you shape your approach to the test. ACT claims that the Math Test is ordered *roughly* by increasing difficulty. We want to emphasize the adverb "roughly" so that you will not be surprised to find an easy question near the end of the test or a difficult one near the beginning.

You should pace yourself according to the knowledge that an early problem on the test will be easier than a problem late in the test. With 60 minutes to solve 60 problems, you might be thinking that you should allot a minute for each problem. But easy problems should take you less than a minute to solve, while solving a difficult problem can be time-consuming. If you find yourself spending too much time on a problem early in the test, skip it, and come back to it later.

That said, you should not rush through the early problems on the test to save time for the problems near the end. Remember that all questions on the ACT are worth the same to the scoring machine, so you should set a pace that allows you to answer the early problems carefully without sacrificing speed.

Work Forward

The best way to approach a math question is initially to ignore the answer choices and to come up with your own answer using the information provided in the question. Coming up with your own answer first is known as "working forward." By formulating an answer on your own, you can avoid being influenced in the wrong direction by incorrect but appealing answer choices. Here's the process for answering questions:

1. Read the question without looking at the answer choices.
2. Understand what the question is asking and have a plan for finding the answer.
3. Answer the question as if there were no answer choices.
4. Match your answer to the answer choices given.
5. Fill in the appropriate bubble on the answer sheet.

Following this method simply insures that you will actively engage with each problem. When you write essays, teachers often tell you to write an outline first, since a quick outline can help you organize your thoughts and actually save you time by letting you see where you need to go. Think of this method as providing you with a tiny outline for each math question. When you read the question and take a moment to make sure you know what it's asking, you are building an outline in your head of how to solve it. In the long run, this will cut down on wrong paths and dead ends and save you time.

Work Backward

We've told you not to look at the answers. Now we're going to amend that advice: You shouldn't look at the answers unless you've taken the time to try to understand a question and you've come to the conclusion that going to the answers and using them to try to answer the question is in fact your best strategy. This is known as "working backward." There are two reasons why you might come to this decision:

1. You think plugging in the answer choices is the best tactic for approaching the question.
2. You're not sure exactly how to answer the question, and you think you can either eliminate all the wrong answers—or at least some of them—by working with the answer choices.

Whatever your reason, make sure you approach the answer choices critically and strategically. Don't let them influence you. Try to see how you can use them.

Take the following example:

A classroom contains 31 chairs, some of which have arms and some of which do not. If the room contains 5 more armchairs than chairs without arms, how many armchairs does it contain?

A. 10
B. 13
C. 16
D. 18
E. 21

Given this question, you could build the equations:

Total chairs (31) = armchairs (x) + normal chairs (y)

Normal chairs (y) = armchairs (x) – 5

Then, since $y = x - 5$ you can make the equation:

$$31 = x + (x - 5)$$
$$31 = 2x - 5$$
$$36 = 2x$$
$$x = 18$$

There are 18 armchairs in the classroom.

This approach of building and working out the equations will produce the right answer, but it takes a long time! What if you strategically plugged in the answer choices instead? Since the numbers ascend in value, let's choose the one in the middle: **C**, 16. This is a smart strategic move because if we plug in 16 and discover that it is too small a number to satisfy the equation, we can eliminate **A** and **B** along with **C**. Alternatively, if 16 is too big, we can eliminate **D** and **E** along with **C**.

So our strategy is in place. Now let's work it out. If you have 16 armchairs, then you would have 11 normal chairs and the room would contain 27 total chairs. We needed the total numbers of chairs to equal 31, so clearly **C** is not the right answer. But because the total number of chairs was too few, you can also eliminate **A** and **B**, the answer choices with smaller numbers of armchairs. If you then plug in **D**, 18, you have 13 normal chairs and 31 total chairs. There's your answer.

In this instance, plugging in the answers takes less time and, in general, just seems easier. Notice that the last sentence began with the words "in this instance." Working backward and plugging in is not always the best method. For some questions, it won't be possible to work backward at all. For the test, you will need to develop a sense of when working backward can most help you. A good rule of thumb for deciding whether to work backward is:

- Work backward when the question describes an equation of some sort, and the answer choices are all simple numbers.

If the answer choices contain variables, working backward will often be quite difficult—more difficult than working out the problem would be. If the answer choices are complicated, with hard fractions or radicals, plugging in might prove so complex that it's a waste of time.

Find the Fastest Route

As we've just discussed, there are often several ways to answer an ACT math question. You can use trial and error; you can set up and solve an equation; and, for some questions, you might be able to answer the question quickly, intuitively, and elegantly, if you can just spot how. These different approaches to answering questions vary in the amount of time they take. Trial and error generally takes the longest, while the flash-of-intuition method either happens very quickly or not at all.

Take, for example, the following problem:

> Which has a greater area, a square with sides measuring 4 cm, or a circle with a radius of the same length?

The obvious way to solve this problem is simply to plug 4 into the formula for the area of a square and the area of a circle. Let's do it: The area of a square is equal to s^2, so the area of this square $= 4^2 = 16$. The area of a circle is equal to πr^2, and the area of this circle must therefore be $\pi \times 4^2 = 16\pi$. Since 16π is obviously bigger than 16, the circle must be bigger. That worked nicely. But a faster approach would have been to draw a quick to-scale diagram with the square and circle superimposed.

An even quicker way would have been to understand the equations of area for a square and a circle so well that it was just *obvious* that the circle was bigger, since the equation for the circle will square the radius and multiply it by π, whereas the equation for the square will only square the radius.

While you may not be able to become a math whiz and just *know* the answer, you can learn to look for a quicker route, such as choosing to draw a diagram instead of working out the equation. As with the example above, a quicker route is not necessarily a less accurate one. Making such choices comes down to practice, an awareness that those other routes are out there, and basic mathematical ability.

The value of time saving strategies is obvious: Less time spent on some questions allows you to devote more time to difficult problems. It is this issue of time that separates the students who ace the math section from those who merely do well. Whether the ability to find accurate shortcuts is an actual measure of mathematical prowess is not for us to say (though we can think of arguments on either side), but the ability to find those shortcuts absolutely matters on this test.

Use Your Math Intuition

So we've told you all about shortcuts, but now we're going to give you some advice that might seem strange: You shouldn't go into every question searching for a shortcut. If you have to search and search for a shortcut, it might end up taking longer than the normal route. If you go into each question knowing there might be a shortcut and keep your mind open as you think about the question, you will find the shortcuts you need.

To some extent, you can teach yourself to recognize when a question might contain a shortcut through practice. For example, from the previous problem, you know that there will probably be a shortcut for all the questions that give you the dimensions of two shapes and ask you to compare them: You can just draw a diagram. A frantic test-taker would see the information given and then rush to the simplest route and work out the equations. But if you are a little calmer, you can see that drawing a diagram is the best idea.

Finally, the fact that we advocate using shortcuts doesn't mean you shouldn't focus on learning how to work out a problem. In fact, we can guarantee that you're not going to find a shortcut for a problem *unless* you know how to work it out the long way. After all, a shortcut is just using your knowledge to see a faster way to answer the question. To put it another way, while we've been using the term "math shortcut," we could just as easily have used the term "math intuition." If you don't have that knowledge base from which to work, you're not going to have anything on which to base your intuition. In contrast, you might be able to figure out an answer by trial and error even if you don't see exactly how to solve the problem.

Set a Target Score

Your strategy on the Math Test, and particularly the extent of your efforts to find shortcuts, should be based on your target score. If you're looking to get a 23 or lower on the Math Test, there simply is no need to go looking for shortcuts. You can get a 23, or even a 25 or 26, without answering a large number of questions, so there's no need to race through the test. You should focus on getting questions right. Of course, you should remain aware that shortcuts exist and use them when you see them, but don't get upset or worried if you're not unearthing a shortcut in every other question.

Students looking to score a 27 or above on the Math Test, though, should *not* be working out every question. Finding quicker ways to answer questions must be part of your strategy, for only through these faster methods will you give yourself the time to get to and answer the last few difficult questions that can make all the difference. On these last few questions, even the best students might very well have to plow their way through using trial and error, and this method takes a bit of time. So you must give yourself that time by moving quickly through the earlier stages of the test.

Be wary: This advice does *not* imply that you should simply work faster; it says that you should look for the shorter but *just as accurate* route to the answer. Do not sacrifice accuracy for speed. If you can find the short but accurate route, great! But if you can't do both, it's always better to answer correctly than to answer quickly. Had enough? Remember these test-taking strategies and use them on the practice sets.

REVIEW FOR THE ACT MATH TEST

As we mentioned in the introduction, the ACT Math Test will evaluate your knowledge of six areas of high school math. The questions are categorized into the following broad topics:

1. Pre-Algebra
2. Elementary Algebra
3. Intermediate Algebra
4. Coordinate Geometry
5. Plane Geometry
6. Trigonometry

Our math review touches on each of these categories. We will explain the math concepts and rules on the ACT tests, and we'll also discuss how the ACT will likely test these topics. So go ahead and read on!

PRE-REVIEW REVIEW

Before diving into the math on the ACT tests, we very quickly want to review the math the ACT assumes you know. The ACT will not explicitly ask questions on these topics, but since the test writers assume that you know them, many questions will indirectly test them.

Order of Operations

You must know the order of operations for the test. The best way to remember which operation gets performed before another is the acronym PEMDAS, which stands for:

Parentheses
Exponents
Multiplication
Division
Addition
Subtraction

If you come across an equation that contains all of these elements, you should first carry out the math within the parentheses, then work out the exponents, then do the multiplication and the division (working from left to right), and finally the addition and subtraction, again working from left to right. For example, take the expression:

$$\frac{(18-3)\times 2^2}{5}-7+(6\times 3-1)$$

You would first work out the math in the parentheses (following PEMDAS even within the parentheses, meaning you should do multiplication before subtraction):

$$\frac{15 \times 2^2}{5} - 7 + 17$$

Then work out the exponents:

$$\frac{15 \times 4}{5} - 7 + 17$$

Then do the multiplication:

$$\frac{60}{5} - 7 + 17$$

Then the division:

$$12 - 7 + 17$$

Then the addition and subtraction:

$$22$$

Odd and Even Numbers

You should know about odd and even numbers and the differences between them. For this topic, however, we will provide a very quick review.

Even Numbers

Even numbers are numbers that are divisible by 2 with no remainder. Remember that 0 is included in this definition.

$$..., -6, -4, -2, 0, 2, 4, 6, ...$$

Odd Numbers

Odd numbers are numbers that, if divided by 2, will leave a remainder of 1.

$$..., -5, -3, -1, 1, 3, 5, ...$$

Operations and Odd and Even Numbers

There are a number of rules regarding operations and odd and even numbers that you should know instinctively.

Addition

+	Odd	Even
Odd	Even	Odd
Even	Odd	Even

Subtraction

−	Odd	Even
Odd	Even	Odd
Even	Odd	Even

Multiplication

×	Odd	Even
Odd	Odd	Even
Even	Even	Even

Signed Numbers

The term "signed numbers" refers to numbers that include either a positive or negative sign, and are therefore marked as being either greater than zero (positive) or less than zero (negative). Zero has no sign.

Students who are comfortable with positive numbers sometimes get confused when dealing with negative numbers. For example, while positive numbers become larger as they move farther away from zero, negative numbers become smaller: –10 is a smaller number than –1. When dealing with negative numbers, be careful not just to see the 10 in –10 and assume that it is a larger number than –1, unless you are dealing with absolute value, which is covered later in this chapter.

Negative Numbers and Operations

Negative numbers behave differently than positive numbers when you perform various operations on them. In terms of addition and subtraction, negative numbers invert the operations.

Adding Signed Numbers

When a negative number is added to another number, the sum will be a smaller number. In fact, adding a negative number is the same as subtracting a positive number of the same absolute value (see p. 43).

$$3 + (-2) = 1, \text{ just as } 3 - 2 = 1$$

Subtracting Signed Numbers

When a negative number is subtracted from another number, the difference will be a larger number. In fact, subtracting a negative number is the same as adding a positive number of the same value.

$$3 - (-2) = 5, \text{ just as } 3 + 2 = 5$$

Multiplying and Dividing with Negative Numbers

Negative numbers also follow sign rules when you multiply or divide them:

× or ÷	Positive	Negative
Positive	Positive	Negative
Negative	Negative	Positive

PRE-ALGEBRA

The various pre-algebra topics are the most basic on the ACT Math Test. You probably covered much of this material in your middle school math classes. These topics are not conceptually difficult, but they do have some nuances you may have forgotten along the way. Also, since questions covering pre-algebra often are not that hard, you should make sure you review properly to get these questions right.

The topics in this section appear roughly in order of frequency on the Math Test. Number problems are usually the most common pre-algebra questions on the test, while series questions are usually the least common.

1. Number Problems
2. Multiples, Factors, and Primes
3. Divisibility and Remainders
4. Percentages, Fractions, and Decimals
5. Ratios and Proportions
6. Mean, Median, and Mode
7. Probability
8. Absolute Value
9. Exponents and Roots
10. Series

While "Multiples, Factors, and Primes" and "Divisibility and Remainders" do not explicitly appear too frequently on the test, the math behind them will help you answer number problems, so we've included them at the top of the list.

We mentioned that the above list is only roughly ordered by decreasing frequency. If it were in an exact order, percentages would share the top billing with number problems; because we wanted to keep related topics close together, we sacrificed a bit of precision.

Number Problems

On the ACT Math Test, number problems are word problems that ask you to manipulate numbers. The math in number problems is usually extremely simple. You are seldom asked to perform operations that are more complicated than basic addition, subtraction, multiplication, and division. Despite the simple operations, number problems can be confusing because of their wording and because of the multiple steps involved in answering them. Here's an example of a typical number problem on the Math Test:

> Train A travels at 90 miles per hour and covers 360 miles. Train B covers the same distance but travels at 60 miles per hour. How much longer does it take Train B than Train A to cover that distance?

The first step in answering these questions is to read carefully to make sure you know exactly what they are asking. Because of the time pressure of the test, some students feel as if the time they take to understand the question is wasted since they aren't actually doing any math. But taking a moment to ask yourself what the question is asking is *crucial*. Not only will you be more likely to get the question right if you take a moment to make sure you understand it, but that little bit of invested time will actually *save* you time later, since you will be able to proceed with an understanding of what you need to do.

The question above asks the difference in time it takes the two trains to cover the same distance. Your first step should be to figure out how long each train takes to travel 360 miles. Once you've done that, you can subtract the smaller number from the bigger number to get the difference in time.

The question gives you two pieces of information that will help you figure out the trains' times: the speed (miles per hour) and the distance (miles). If you divide the distance by the speed, you will cancel out the miles and end up with the hours:

$$\text{Time (hours)} = \frac{\text{distance (miles)}}{\text{speed (miles/hour)}}$$

Once you've done that, you'll see that Train A travels for 4 hours and Train B for 6 hours:

$$6 \text{ hours} - 4 \text{ hours} = 2 \text{ hours}$$

Multiples, Factors, and Primes

Multiples, factors, and primes appear quite frequently on the ACT Math Test. You will rarely see a non-word problem covering multiples, factors, and primes; this topic almost always appears in word problem form.

While these questions are relatively easy, they can be quite confusing simply because of the terminology they use. Below, we give you the definition for each of these three mathematical concepts.

Multiples

The multiple of a number is the product generated when that number is multiplied by an integer. The first five multiples of 7 are 7, 14, 21, 28, and 35 since $7 \times 1 = 7$, $7 \times 2 = 14$, $7 \times 3 = 21$, $7 \times 4 = 28$, and $7 \times 5 = 35$.

The Least Common Multiple

The least common multiple (LCM) is the name given to the lowest multiple that two particular numbers share. For example, the multiples of 6 and 8 are:

- **Multiples of 6:** 6, 12, 18, **24**, 30, 36, 42, **48**, 54, . . .
- **Multiples of 8:** 8, 16, **24**, 32, 40, **48**, 56, 64, 72, . . .

As the two lists show, 6 and 8 both have 24 and 48 as multiples (they also share many other multiples, such as 72, 96, etc.). Because 24 is the lowest in value of these shared multiples, it is the least common multiple of 6 and 8.

Being able to figure out the least common multiple of two numbers can prove quite handy on the ACT, especially for questions in which you have to add or subtract two fractions with unlike denominators (we'll explain when we talk about fractions).

Factors

A factor of a number is an integer that divides evenly into the number. For example, 6, 4, 3, and 2 are all factors of 12 because $\frac{12}{6} = 2, \frac{12}{4} = 3, \frac{12}{3} = 4,$ and $\frac{12}{2} = 6$. Factors, then, are related to multiples. A given number is a multiple of all of its factors: 2 and 6 are factors of 12, so 12 is a multiple of both 2 and 6.

The Greatest Common Factor

The greatest common factor (GCF) of two numbers is the largest factor that the two numbers share. For example, the GCF of 18 and 24 is 6, since 6 is the largest number that is a factor of both 18 and 24.

Factorization

To find all the factors of a number, write them down in pairs, beginning with 1 and the number you're factoring. We'll factor 24 for this example. So, 1 and 24 are both factors of 24. Next, try every integer greater than 1 in increasing order. Here are the factor pairs we find for 24: 1 and 24, 2 and 12, 3 and 8, and 4 and 6.

You know you've found all the factors of a number when the increasing integer in each pair exceeds the decreasing integer. For example, after you found that 4 was a factor of 24 and 5 was not, you would see that 6, the next factor of 24, had already been included in a pair of factors. Thus, all the factors have been found.

As you might imagine, factoring a very large number can get pretty involved. But don't worry—that kind of extensive factoring won't be asked of you on the test.

Primes

A prime number is divisible by only 1 and itself (the number 1 itself is not considered prime). For example, 17 is prime because it is divisible by only 1 and 17. The first few primes, in increasing order, are:

$$2, 3, 5, 7, 11, 13, 17, 19, 23, 29, 31, 37, 41, 43, 47, 53, \ldots$$

Prime Factorization

Another form of factorization is called prime factorization. Prime factorization expresses an integer as the product of a series of prime numbers.

To find the prime factorization of a number, divide it and all of its factors until every integer remaining is prime. This group of prime numbers is the prime factorization of the original integer. Let's find the prime factorization of 36 as an example:

$$36 = 2 \times 18 = 2 \times 2 \times 9 = 2 \times 2 \times 3 \times 3$$

As you may already have noticed, there is more than one way to find the prime factorization of a number. We could have first resolved 36 into 6×6, for example, and then determined the prime factorization from there. So don't worry—you can't screw up. No matter which path you take, you will always get the same result—that is, as long as you do your arithmetic correctly.

Just for practice, let's find a couple more prime factorizations:

$$45 = 3 \times 15 = 3 \times 3 \times 5$$
$$41 = 1 \times 41$$

Since the only factors of 41 are 1 and 41, it is a prime number. In other words, 41 is its own prime factorization.

Relatively Prime Numbers

Two numbers are called relatively prime if they share no common prime factors (i.e., if their GCF is 1). This doesn't necessarily mean, however, that each number is itself prime. For instance, 8 and 15 are relatively prime because they have no common primes in their prime factorizations ($8 = 2 \times 2 \times 2$ and $15 = 3 \times 5$), but neither number is prime. It is a good idea just to know the definition of relatively prime numbers, in case the concept pops up on the test somewhere.

Divisibility and Remainders

Divisibility and remainders are also popular subjects for pre-algebraic number problems on the ACT Math Test. As with multiples, factors, and primes, you will probably not see basic problems on divisibility and remainders, but the topic will appear in relatively complicated word problems.

A number (x) is divisible by another number (y) if, when x is divided by y, the answer is a whole number. For example, 6 is divisible by 3 because $\frac{6}{3} = 2$, and 2 is a whole number. However, 6 is not divisible by 4 because $\frac{6}{4} = 1\frac{2}{4}$, which is not a whole number. Another way of describing $\frac{6}{4}$ is to say that you can make one complete division with a remainder of 2.

To check divisibility, it is always possible to do the division by hand and see whether the result is a whole number. However, if the number we are dividing is large, this becomes very difficult. There are some divisibility rules that make this task much easier—these rules allow us to determine whether a number is divisible by another number without having to carry out the division.

Divisibility Rules

1. All whole numbers are divisible by 1.
2. All numbers with a ones digit of 0, 2, 4, 6, and 8 are divisible by 2.
3. A number is divisible by 3 if its digits add up to a number divisible by 3. For example, 6,711 is divisible by 3 because 6 + 7 + 1 + 1 = 15, and 15 is divisible by 3.
4. A number is divisible by 4 if its last two digits are divisible by 4. For example, 78,052 is divisible by 4 because 52 is divisible by 4. But 7,850 is not divisible by 4 because 50 is not divisible by 4.
5. A number is divisible by 5 if it ends in 0 or 5.
6. A number is divisible by 6 if it is even and also divisible by 3.
7. Sorry. There are no rules for 7.
8. A number is divisible by 8 if its last three digits are divisible by 8. For example, 905,256 is divisible by 8 because 256 is divisible by 8. But 74,513 is not divisible by 8 because 513 is not divisible by 8.
9. A number is divisible by 9 if its digits add up to a number divisible by 9. For example, 1,458 is divisible by 9 because 1 + 4 + 5 + 8 = 18, and 18 is divisible by 9.
10. A number is divisible by 10 if it ends in 0.

Two Notes: (1) Because a number divided by itself always yields 1, a number is always divisible by itself. For example, 7 is divisible by 7, and 8,374 is divisible by 8,374. (2) No number is divisible by a number greater than itself.

Remainders

A remainder is the number that remains after x has been divided by y. If y divides evenly into x, the remainder of $x \div y$ is zero. A remainder will always be smaller than the number that is doing the dividing. For instance, if you divide 22 by 5, your answer is 4 with a remainder of 2.

Percentages, Fractions, and Decimals

Percentage problems appear frequently on the ACT Math Test. Because percentages are essentially fractions and decimals, our review of percentages will begin with a review of fractions and decimals. While questions dealing specifically with fractions and decimals *per se* are rare on the ACT Math Test, knowing more about them will aid your understanding of the more common questions about percentages.

Fractions

Although you may not see a fraction problem on the Math Test (or, at most, you'll see one or two), you should still review your knowledge of fractions, as they form the basis for percentages, a favorite topic of the ACT.

A fraction describes a part of a whole. The number on the bottom of the fraction is called the denominator, and it denotes how many equal parts the whole is divided into. The number on the top of the fraction is called the numerator, and it denotes how many of the parts we are taking. For example, the fraction $\frac{3}{4}$ denotes "three of four equal parts," 3 being the numerator and 4 being the denominator. You can also think of fractions as similar to division. In fact, $\frac{3}{4}$ has the same value as $3 \div 4$.

The ACT may indirectly test your ability to add, subtract, multiply, and divide fractions. Questions that deal more directly with fractions will probably test your ability to reduce and compare fractions.

Adding and Subtracting Fractions

There are two different types of fractions that you may have to add or subtract: Those with the same denominator, and those with different denominators.

If fractions have the same denominator, adding them is extremely easy. All you have to do is add up the numerators:

$$\frac{1}{20} + \frac{3}{20} + \frac{13}{20} = \frac{17}{20}$$

Subtraction works similarly. If the denominators of the fractions are equal, then you simply subtract one numerator from the other:

$$\frac{13}{20} - \frac{2}{20} = \frac{11}{20}$$

If the fractions do not have equal denominators, the process is somewhat more involved. The first step is to make the denominators the same. To set the denominators of two fractions as equal, find the least common denominator (LCD), which is simply the least common multiple of the two denominators. For example, 18 is the LCD of $\frac{1}{6}$ and $\frac{4}{9}$, since 18 is the smallest multiple of both 6 and 9.

Setting the denominators of two fractions equal to one another is a two-step process. First, find the LCD. Second, write each fraction as an equivalent fraction with the LCD as the new denominator, remembering to multiply the numerator by the same multiple as the denominator. For example, if you wanted to add $\frac{5}{12}$ and $\frac{4}{9}$, you would do the following:

First, find the LCD:

1. Factor the denominators: $12 = 2 \times 2 \times 3$, and $9 = 3 \times 3$.
2. Find the LCM of the denominators: $2 \times 2 \times 3 \times 3 = 36$.
3. The LCD is 36.

Once you've found the LCD, write each fraction as an equivalent fraction with the LCD as the new denominator. Multiply the denominator of the first fraction by an integer to get the LCD. Multiply the numerator by the same integer.

$$\text{Denominator} = 12 \times 3 = 36$$
$$\text{Numerator} = 5 \times 3 = 15$$

The new first fraction is, therefore, $\frac{15}{36}$.

Multiply the denominator and numerator of the second fraction by an integer to get the LCD. Multiply the numerator by the same integer.

$$\text{Denominator} = 9 \times 4 = 36$$
$$\text{Numerator} = 4 \times 4 = 16$$

The new second fraction is, therefore, $\frac{16}{36}$.

Now that the fractions have the same denominator, you can quickly add the numerators to get the final answer: $15 + 16 = 31$, so the answer is $\frac{31}{36}$.

Multiplying Fractions

Multiplying fractions is quite easy. Simply multiply the numerators together and multiply the denominators together, as seen in the example below:

$$\frac{4}{5} \times \frac{2}{7} \times \frac{1}{3} = \frac{4 \times 2 \times 1}{5 \times 7 \times 3} = \frac{8}{105}$$

Dividing Fractions

Multiplication and division are inverse operations. It makes sense, then, that to perform division with fractions, all you have to do is invert (flip over) the dividing fraction and then multiply:

$$\frac{1}{4} \div \frac{5}{8} = \frac{1}{4} \times \frac{8}{5} = \frac{8}{20}$$

Note that just as multiplication by a fraction smaller than one results in a *smaller* product, division by a fraction smaller than one results in a *larger* product.

Reducing Fractions

If you encounter fractions involving large, unwieldy numbers, such as $\frac{18}{102}$, the best move is usually to see if the fraction can be reduced to smaller numbers.

The fastest way to simplify a fraction is to divide both the numerator and denominator by their greatest common factor. In the case of $\frac{18}{102}$, the GCF of 18 and 102 is 6, leaving you with $\frac{3}{17}$. With your knowledge of divisibility rules, you should be able to see that both the numerator and denominator are divisible by 6. Had you not immediately seen that 6 was the greatest common factor, you could have divided both numbers by 2 and gotten $\frac{9}{51}$.

From there, it would have been pretty obvious that both the numerator and denominator are also divisible by 3, yielding $\frac{3}{17}$.

The ACT might also present you with variables in fraction form and ask you to reduce them. You can reduce these variable fractions as long as you can find like factors in both the numerator and denominator. For example, to reduce this fraction,

$$\frac{6x^2 + 2}{4x}$$

you merely have to notice that all of the terms in both the numerator and denominator contain 2 as a factor. Dividing 2 out of the fraction, you get:

$$\frac{3x^2 + 1}{2x}$$

Comparing Fractions

The rare fraction problem you see may ask you to compare two fractions. If either the denominators or the numerators of the two fractions are the same, that comparison is easy. For example, $\frac{8}{9}$ is obviously greater than $\frac{5}{9}$, just as $\frac{5}{9}$, is greater than $\frac{5}{17}$. Just remember, if the numerators are the same, the greater fraction is the one with the smaller denominator.

If the two fractions don't lend themselves to easy comparison, there is still a quick and easy method that will allow you to make the comparison: cross multiplication. To do this, multiply the numerator of each fraction by the denominator of the other. Write the product of each multiplication next to the numerator you used to calculate it. The greater product will be next to the greater fraction. For example:

$$32 = \frac{4}{7} \,\,{>}\!\!\times\!\!{<}\,\, \frac{5}{8} = 35$$

Since 35, the greater product, is written next to $\frac{5}{8}$, that is the greater fraction.

Decimals

Decimals are simply another way to express fractions. To get a decimal, divide the numerator of a fraction by the denominator. For example, if you take the fraction $\frac{2}{5}$ and divide 2 by 5, you get 0.4. Therefore the decimal 0.4 is equal to $\frac{2}{5}$.

Questions testing decimals almost never appear on the ACT. If decimal numbers do appear and you have to add, subtract, multiply, or divide them, the best thing to do is to use a calculator.

Percentages

Percentage problems always make an appearance on the ACT Math Test. You will probably see at least two per test. Percentages are just another way to talk about a specific type of fraction. Percent literally means "of 100." If you have 25 percent of all the money in the world, that means you have $\frac{25}{100}$ of the world's money.

Let's take the question "4 is what percent of 20?" This question presents you with a whole, 20, and then asks you to determine how much of that whole 4 represents in percentage form, which means "of 100." To come to the answer, you have to set up an equation that sets the fraction $\frac{4}{20}$ equal to $\frac{x}{100}$:

$$\frac{4}{20} \; \diagdown\!\!\!\times\!\!\!\diagup \; \frac{x}{100}$$

If you then cross multiply to solve for x, you get $20x = 400$, meaning $x = 20$. Therefore, 4 is 20 percent of 20. You also might realize that instead of working out all this cross multiplication, you could simply do the following:

$$\frac{4}{20} \times 100 = 20$$

Important Percentage Terms

Percentage terminology can be a little tricky, so here is a short glossary of terms:

- **Percent more:** if one person has 50 percent more children than a second person, then that first person has the same amount as the second person, plus 50 percent of the amount the second person has.
- **Percent increase:** percent increase means the same thing as percent more. If the price of some item increases 10 percent, the new price is the original plus 10 percent of that original—in other words, 110 percent of the original.
- **Percent decrease:** the opposite of percent increase. This term means you subtract the specified percent of the original value from that original.

Sometimes students see these terms and figure out what the 10 percent increase or decrease is, but then forget to carry out the necessary addition or subtraction. Here's a sample ACT percentage problem:

A shirt originally cost $20, but during a sale its price was reduced by 15%. What is the current price of the shirt?

A. $3
B. $5
C. $13
D. $17
E. $23

In this question, you are told the whole, $20, and the percentage, 15%, and you need to figure out the part. You can therefore quickly set up the equation (once you are comfortable with percentages you might be able to skip this step of setting up the equation and move straight to solving for x):

$$\frac{x}{20} = .15$$

You can find x by multiplying 20 by .15 to see what the change in price was:

$$x = 20 \times .15 = 3$$

Once you know the price change, you then need to subtract it from the original price, since the question asks for the reduced price of the shirt.

$$\$20 - \$3 = \$17$$

The answer is **D**. Notice that if you had only finished the first part of this solution and had looked at the answer choices, you might have seen that $3 hanging out at answer **A** like a big affirmation of correctness and been tempted into choosing it without finishing the question. You could also solve this problem in one step by realizing that if the sale price was 15% lower than the original, it was 85% of the original. Therefore, $0.85($20) = $17.

Double Percentages

Some ACT questions will ask you to determine a percent of a percent. Take this question:

> The original price of a banana in a store is $2. During a sale, the store reduces the price by 25% and Joe buys the banana. Joe then meets his friend, Sam, who is almost faint with hunger. Seeing an opportunity, Joe raises the price of the banana 10% from the price at which he bought it, and sells it to Sam. How much does Sam pay?

In this question, you are asked to determine the cumulative effect of two percentage changes. The key to solving this type of problem is to realize that each percentage change is dependent on the last. In other words, you have to work out the effect of the first percentage change, come up with a value, and then use that value to determine the effect of the second percentage change.

In the problem asked above, you would first find 25% of the original price.

$$\frac{25}{100} \times \$2 = \frac{50}{100} = \$.50$$

Now subtract that $.50 from the original price.

$$\$2 - \$.5 = \$1.50$$

Then we find 10% of $1.50:

$$\frac{10}{100} \times \$1.50 = \frac{15}{100} = \$.15$$

Therefore, Sam buys the banana at a price of $1.50 + $.15 = $1.65.

When you are working on a percentage problem that involves a series of percentage changes, you should follow the same procedure you would for one single percentage change at each stage of the series. For the first percentage change, figure out what the whole is, calculate the percentage of the whole, and make sure to perform addition or subtraction, if necessary. Then take the new value and put it through these same steps for the second percentage change.

Ratios and Proportions

On the typical ACT Math Test, you'll see a couple of problems dealing with proportions or ratios.

Ratios

Ratios can look a lot like fractions, and they are related to fractions, but they differ in important ways. Whereas a fraction describes a part out of a whole, a ratio compares two separate parts of the same whole.

A ratio can be written in a variety of ways. Mathematically it can appear as $\frac{3}{1}$ or as 3:1. In words, it should be written out as "the ratio of three to one." Each of these three forms of this ratio means the same thing: There are three of one thing for every one of another. If you have three red marbles and one blue marble, then the ratio of red marbles to blue marbles is 3:1. For the ACT, you must remember that ratios compare parts to parts, rather than parts to a whole. For example:

> Of every 40 games a baseball team plays, it loses 12 games. What is the ratio of the team's losses to wins?
>
> **A.** 3:10
> **B.** 7:10
> **C.** 3:7
> **D.** 7:3
> **E.** 10:3

This ratio question is a little tricky because the information is stated in terms of whole to part, but the question asks for a part to part answer. The problem tells you that the team loses 12 of every 40 games, but it asks you for the ratio of losses to wins, not losses to games. So the first thing you have to figure out is how many times the team wins in 40 games:

$$14 - 12 = 28$$

The team wins 28 of every 40 games. So for every 12 losses, the team has 28 wins, or 12:28. You can reduce this ratio by dividing both sides by 4, to get 3 losses for every 7 wins, or 3:7. So **C** is correct. However, if you didn't realize that losses to games was part to whole, you might have just reduced the ratio 12:40 to 3:10, and then picked **A**.

Proportions

If you have a ratio of 3 red marbles to 1 blue marble, that doesn't necessarily mean that you have exactly 3 red marbles and 1 blue one. It could also mean that you have 6 red and 2 blue marbles, or that you have 240 red and 80 blue marbles. In other words, ratios compare only *relative size*. In order to determine how many of each color of marbles you actually have, you need to know how many total marbles you have in addition to knowing the ratio.

The ACT will occasionally ask questions testing your ability to figure out a quantity given the ratio between items and the total number of all the items. For example:

> You have red, blue, and green marbles in the ratio of 5:4:3, and you have a total of 36 marbles. How many blue marbles do you have?

The information given states that for each group of 5 red marbles, you have a corresponding group of 4 blue marbles and a group of 3 green marbles. The ratio therefore tells you that out of every 12 marbles (since 12 = 5 + 4 + 3), 4 of them will be blue. The question also tells you that you have 36 total marbles.

Since we know that the ratio will not change no matter how many marbles you have, we can solve this problem by setting up a proportion, which is an equation that states that two ratios are equal. In this case, we are going to equate 4:12 and x:36, with x being the number of blue marbles that we would have if we had 36 total marbles. To do math with proportions, it is most useful to set up the proportions in fraction form:

$$\frac{4}{12} = \frac{x}{36}$$

Now you just need to isolate x by cross-multiplying:

$$12x = 4 \times 36$$
$$12x = 144$$
$$x = 12$$

Mean, Median, and Mode

The arithmetic mean, median, and mode are all different ways to describe a group, or set, of numbers. On the ACT, you'll most likely see questions dealing with the arithmetic mean, but you should be prepared for median and mode questions as well.

Arithmetic Mean (a.k.a. Average)

The arithmetic mean, which is also called the average, is the most important and most commonly tested of these three mathematical concepts. The basic rules for finding an average are not very complicated. To find the average of a set of n numbers, you need to find the sum of all the numbers and divide that sum by n.

For example, the mean of the set 9, 8, 13, 10 is:

$$\frac{9+8+13+10}{4} = \frac{40}{4} = 10$$

Many ACT problems about mean will be straightforward, giving you a bunch of numbers and asking you to find their average. But some problems will be presented in a more roundabout fashion. For instance, the ACT might give you three numbers of a four-number set as well as the average of that set, and ask you to find the fourth number, like so:

> If the average of four numbers is 22, and three of the numbers are 7, 11, and 18, then what is the fourth number?

To solve this type of problem, you have to realize that if you know the average of a group, and also know how many numbers are in the group, you can calculate the sum of the numbers in the group. In the question asked above, you know that the average of the numbers is 22 and that there are four numbers. This means that the four numbers, when added together, must equal 4 × 22, which is 88. Now, from the information given in the problem and our own calculations, we know three of the four numbers in the set and the total sum of the numbers in the set:

$$7 + 11 + 18 + \text{unknown number} = 88$$

Solving for the unknown number is easy: All you have to do is subtract 7, 11, and 18 from 88 to get 52, which is the answer.

Median

The median is the number whose value is in the middle of the numbers in a particular set. Take the set 6, 19, 3, 11, 7. If we arrange the numbers in order of value, we get:

$$3, 6, 7, 11, 19$$

When we list the numbers in this way, it becomes clear that the middle number in this group is 7, making 7 the median.

The set we just looked at contained an odd number of items, but in a set with an even number of items it's impossible to isolate a single number as the median. Let's add one number to the set from the previous example:

$$3, 6, 7, 11, 15, 19$$

In this case, we find the median by taking the two numbers in the middle and finding their average. The two middle numbers in this set are 7 and 11, so the median of the set is $\frac{(7+11)}{2} = 9$.

Mode

The mode is the number within a set that appears most frequently. In the set 10, 11, 13, 11, 20, the mode is 11 since that number appears twice and all the others appear just once. In a set where all the numbers appear an equal number of times, there is no mode.

Probability

A typical ACT Math Test asks one question on probability. To begin to deal with these questions, you first have to understand what probability is:

$$\frac{\text{chance of a particular outcome}}{\text{total number of possible outcomes}}$$

For example, let's say you're on a game show and are shown three doors. Behind one door there is a prize, while behind the other two doors sit big piles of nothing. The probability that you will choose the door with the prize is $\frac{1}{3}$, because out of the total three possibilities there is one chance to pick the lucrative door.

Here's an example of a probability question:

> Joe has 3 green marbles, 2 red marbles, and 5 blue marbles. If all the marbles are dropped into a dark bag, what is the probability that Joe will pick out a green marble?

There are three ways for Joe to pick a green marble (since there are three different green marbles), but there are 10 total possible outcomes (one for each marble in the bag). Therefore, the probability of picking a green marble is:

$$\text{Probability} = \frac{\text{particular outcome}}{\text{total outcomes}} = \frac{\text{green marbles}}{\text{total marbles}} = \frac{3}{10} \text{ or } 33\%$$

When you calculate probability, always be careful to divide by the total number of possible outcomes. In the last example, you may have been tempted to leave out the three chances of picking a green marble from the total possibilities, yielding the equation $P = \frac{3}{7}$. If you did that, you'd be wrong.

Absolute Value

The absolute value of a number is its magnitude, regardless of sign. Absolute value is indicated by two vertical lines that surround the number: $|5|$ and $|-5|$, for example. The absolute value of positive five is equal to five: $|5| = 5$. The absolute value of negative five is also equal to five: $|-5| = 5$. Simply remove the sign before the number to produce its absolute value.

On the ACT, you will generally be asked to do a simple addition, subtraction, multiplication, or division problem using the absolute values of numbers. For example,

$$|-4| + |2| = ?$$

Remember that the vertical lines mean you simply ignore the sign, so the question actually looks like this: $4 + 2 = 6$.

Exponents and Roots

At most, you'll see one problem on the ACT Math Test dealing with exponents or roots. It's quite likely you won't see any, but you're still doing yourself a favor by preparing for them.

Exponents

Exponents are a shorthand method of describing how many times a particular number is multiplied by itself. To write $3 \times 3 \times 3 \times 3 \times 3$ in exponent form, we would simply count how many threes were being multiplied together (in this case, five), and then write 3^5. In verbal form, 3^5 is stated as "three to the fifth power."

Raising an Exponent to an Exponent

Occasionally, a question might ask you to raise a power to a power, in the following format: $(3^2)^4$. In such cases, multiply the exponents:

$$(3^2)^4 = 3^{(2 \times 4)} = 3^8$$

If you have an expression involving a variable, like $2a^2$, and you raise it to the third power, then you would write $(2a^2)^3$. To simplify this expression, you would multiply the exponents and raise 2 to the third power; the end result would be $8a^6$. Most basic calculators have an exponent or y^x function key. Be sure to know how to use this function on your calculator before the test.

Square Roots

The square root of a number is the number that, when squared (multiplied by itself), is equal to the given number. For example, the square root of 16 is 4, because $4^2 = 4 \times 4 = 16$. A perfect square is a number whose square root is an integer.

The sign denoting a square root is $\sqrt{}$. To use the previous example, $\sqrt{16} = 4$. Again, be sure to find and know how to use the square-root function, or $\sqrt{}$ key, on your calculator.

Cube Roots

The cube root of a number is the number that, when cubed (raised to the third power), is equal to the given number. The cube root of 8 is 2, because $2 \times 2 \times 2 = 8$.

The sign denoting a cube root is $\sqrt[3]{}$.

Series

Series questions are pretty rare on the ACT. Every once in a while they do pop up, though. A series is a sequence of numbers that proceed one after another, according to some pattern. Usually the ACT will give you a few numbers in a series and ask you to specify what number should come next. For example,

$$-1, 2, -4, 8, -16$$

is a series in which each number is multiplied by –2 to yield the next number; 32 is the next number in the series. This type of question asks you to be able to recognize patterns and then apply them. There isn't one tried-and-true way to find a pattern. Just think critically, and use your intuition and trial and error.

ELEMENTARY ALGEBRA

Unlike the section on pre-algebra, we've organized this elementary algebra section in terms of increasing difficulty:

1. Substitution
2. Simplifying Algebraic Expressions
3. Writing Expressions and Equations
4. Solving Linear Equations
5. Multiplying Binomials
6. Inequalities

This is also the order of the topics in terms of decreasing frequency on the test, with one exception: Problems involving inequalities pop up more often than problems involving binomial multiplication.

Before covering these topics, however, we will address a question brought up by the teachings of some other test prep companies.

To Algebra or Not to Algebra

There are many ways to answer most algebra problems. You can use algebra—setting up and working out equations—or you can plug numbers into equations to try and avoid using algebra. In some cases, you might even be able to solve a question by being a particularly intuitive genius and finding a magnificent shortcut.

We want to stress that none of these methods is necessarily better than another. Which method is best for you depends on your math ability and your target score. Trying to solve problems with algebra is more conceptually demanding, but can take less time. Plugging in numbers makes questions easier to understand, but will likely take more time. In general, if you are uncomfortable with algebra, you should try to use the plugging-in method. If you are comfortable with algebra, using it is probably the best way to go. Still, these suggestions are not carved in stone. If you are generally comfortable with algebra but come upon a question that is stumping you, try plugging in answers. If you usually prefer plugging in answers but come upon a question you can answer using algebra, use algebra. When you study your practice tests and look at the algebra questions you got wrong, you should think about the method you employed. Did you plug in when you should have used algebra? Did you use algebra when you should have plugged in? As for being an intuitive math genius, it just can't be taught—though we will show you how one might think.

Here's a sample algebra question:

A man flipped a coin 162 times. The coin landed with the heads side up 62 more times than it landed with tails up. How many times did the coin land heads?

A. 100
B. 104
C. 108
D. 112
E. 116

Solving by Plugging In

If you were to answer this problem by plugging in numbers, you would pick the middle number or **C**, 108, as the first number to try, since if it does not happen to be the answer, you can discard the numbers smaller than it or larger than it. If the coin came up heads 108 times, then how many times did it land tails? It landed tails 162 – 108 = 54 times. Is 108 heads landings 62 more than 54 tails landings? No, 108 – 54 = 54. In order for the problem to work out, you need more heads landings. You can eliminate **A** and **B** as possibilities. Let's say we choose **D**, 112, as our next plug-in number: 162 – 112 = 50. Does 112 – 50 = 62? Yes. **D** is the answer.

Solving with Algebra

If you answer this question with algebra, you realize that if heads are represented by the variable x, then tails are represented by $(x - 62)$. Therefore:

$$x+(x-62)=162$$
$$2x-62=162$$
$$2x=224$$
$$x=112$$

As you can see, there's simply less math to do for this problem when you use algebra. Using algebra will only take you longer than plugging in if you have trouble coming up with the equation $x + (x - 62) = 162$.

Therefore, if you can quickly come up with the necessary equation, then use algebra to solve algebra problems. If you have the feeling that it will take you a while to figure out the correct equation, then plug in.

Solving by Being an Amazing Genius

It is quite possible that you just looked at this problem and said to yourself, "Other than the 62 more heads, all the other flips were equally heads and tails. So if you take the 62 out of the total of 162, then you know that the other 100 flips were 50 heads and 50 tails. Now I can just add $62 + 50 = 112$. Man, I am an amazing genius!"

The Bottom Line on Using Algebra

Hopefully, our example has convinced you that there isn't any "right way" to answer a question dealing with algebra. There are faster ways and slower ways, and it always benefits you to use the faster way if you can, but the most important thing is getting the question right. Therefore, when you come to a question, don't insist on using only one method to try to answer it. Just do what you have to do in order to answer the question correctly in as little time as possible.

Now we'll begin to cover the topics of elementary algebra tested on the ACT.

Substitution

Substitution questions are the simplest algebra problems on the ACT. These questions provide you with an algebraic expression and the value of a variable within the equation, and ask you to calculate the value of the equation. For example:

> If $2y + 8x = 11$, what is the value of $3(2y + 8x)$?

You might see this question with all its variables and panic. But, in truth, this is a simple problem. Since $2y + 8x = 11$, all you have to do is substitute 11 for $2y + 8x$ in the expression $3(2y + 8x)$, and you get $3(11) = 33$.

For some substitution questions, you will have to do some simple math either before or after the substitution.

Math before Substitution

> If $3x - 7 = 8$, then $23 - 3x =$

In this problem you have to find what $3x$ equals before you can substitute that value into the expression $23 - 3x$. To find $3x$, take:

$$3x - 7 = 8$$

and add 7 to both sides, getting:

$$3x = 15$$

Now we can substitute that 15 into $23 - 3x$:

$$23 - 15 = 8$$

Math after Substitution

If $a + b = 7$ and $b = 3$, then $4a =$

Here we first have to solve for a by substituting the 3 in for b:

$$a + b = 7$$
$$a + 3 = 7$$
$$a = 4$$

Once you know that $a = 4$, just substitute it into $4a$:

$$4 \times 4 = 16$$

Simplifying Algebraic Expressions

Some ACT Math questions test your ability to simplify or manipulate algebraic expressions. To master either of these skills, you must be able to see how an equation might be expressed differently without changing the value of the expression in any way. There are two primary ways to simplify an equation: factoring and combining like terms.

Factoring and Unfactoring

Factoring an algebraic expression means finding factors common to all terms in an expression and dividing them out. For example, to factor $3a + 3b$, you simply divide out the 3 to get $3(a + b)$. Below are some more examples of factoring:

1. $6y + 8x = 2(3y + 4x)$
2. $8b + 24 = 8(b + 3)$
3. $3(x + y) + 4(x + y) = (3 + 4)(x + y) = 7(x + y)$
4. $\dfrac{2x + y}{x} = \dfrac{2x}{x} + \dfrac{y}{x} = 2 + \dfrac{y}{x}$

Unfactoring involves taking a factored expression, such as $8(b + 3)$, and distributing one term to the other(s): $8b + 24$.

Combining Similar Terms

If an expression contains "like terms," you can combine those terms and simplify the equation. "Like terms" refers to identical variables that have the same exponent value.

For example:

You can combine:
$$x^2 + 8x^2 = 9x^2$$
$$y^{13} + 754y^{13} = 755y^{13}$$
$$m^3 + m^3 = 2m^3$$

As long as two terms have the same variable and the same exponent value, you can combine them. Note that when you combine like terms, the variable doesn't change. If two terms have different variables, or the exponent value is different, the terms are not "like terms," and you cannot combine them.

You can't combine: $x^4 + x^2$ or $y^2 + x^2$

Writing Expressions and Equations

Occasionally, the ACT will throw you a word problem that describes an algebraic expression. You will have to write out the expression in numerical form and perhaps simplify it. For example:

> Mary poured g cups of water into a bucket, leaving the bucket with a total of f cups in it. Mary then removed $(g - 3)$ cups of water from the bucket. How many cups of water remain in the bucket?

To answer this question, you have to interpret the word problem. In other words, you have to figure out what is important in the word problem and how it fits into the expression you need to build. This question asks you to generate an expression that describes how many cups of water there are in the bucket *after* Mary removes $(g - 3)$ cups. It doesn't matter what g actually equals because we don't care how much water was in the bucket before Mary added g cups.

To work out the equation, we take the original number of cups in the bucket and subtract from it what was removed:

$$f - (g - 3) = f - g + 3$$

Solving Linear Equations

The most common and foolproof way to solve linear equations is to isolate the variable whose value you are trying to determine on one side of the equation.

If you stay alert, you may also be able to find shortcuts that will greatly reduce your time spent per question without affecting your accuracy. Let's look at an easy example:

> If $6p + 2 = 20$, then $6p - 3 =$

This is an easy problem to solve through the normal algebraic method. First we solve for p:

$$6p + 2 = 20$$
$$6p = 18$$
$$p = 3$$

Next, we plug 3 into the second equation:

$$6p - 3 =$$
$$6(3) - 3 =$$
$$18 - 3 = 15$$

But there's a faster way to answer this question. The secret is that you don't have to solve for p at all. Instead, notice that both equations contain $6p$ and that the value of $6p$ will not change. Therefore, all you have to do in the first equation is solve for $6p$. And as you can see above, that simply means subtracting 2 from 20 to get 18. Once you know $6p$ is 18, you can plug 18 in for $6p$ in the second equation and get your answer.

When you come upon an algebra question asking you to solve an equation, you should always take a second to look for shortcuts. Look for equations that not only have the same variables, but also the same coefficients attached to that variable (such as $6p$ and $6p$). If you are able to find a good shortcut, your knowledge of algebra will save you time.

Multiplying Binomials

A binomial is an algebraic expression consisting of two terms combined by a plus or minus sign. For instance, $x + 4$ and $y - 11$ are both binomials. Multiplying binomials is not a difficult task if you remember the acronym FOIL, which stands for FIRST OUTER INNER LAST. For example, say you are asked to multiply the binomials:

$$(x + 2)(x + 3)$$

You start by multiplying the first number in each polynomial $(x)(x)$, then the outer numbers $(x)(3)$, then the inner numbers $(2)(x)$, and finally the last numbers $(2)(3)$:

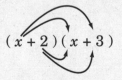

and you get:

$$x^2 + 3x + 2x + 6 = x^2 + 5x + 6$$

The only tricky part to following FOIL is remembering to pay attention to signs. For instance, if you have the polynomials $(x + 2)(x - 3)$, then the -3 comes to play an important part. You always add up the products of FOIL, but look what happens when there's a negative number involved:

$$(x+2)(x-3) = x^2 + 2x + (-3x) + (-6) = x^2 + 2x - 3x - 6$$
$$= x^2 - x - 6$$

There are three equations involving binomial multiplication that you should know backward and forward before you take the ACT, the most important being the first:

$$(x+y)(x-y) = x^2 - y^2$$
$$(x+y)(x+y) = x^2 + 2xy + y^2$$
$$(x-y)(x-y) = x^2 - 2xy + y^2$$

Inequalities

An equation states that the quantities on either side of the equal sign are of the same value. An inequality states that one side of the equation is greater than the other: $a < b$ states that a is less than b, and $a > b$ states that a is greater than b. In other cases, $a \geq b$ means that a is less than or equal to b, while $a \geq b$ means that a is greater than or equal to b.

Solving an inequality is basically the same as solving a normal equation: All the rules of simplification and having to do the same thing to both sides still apply. The one rule that does differ when working with inequalities comes when you multiply or divide both sides by a negative. If you do so, you must flip the sign: If $x > y$, then $-x < -y$. For example, if you have $2x + 6 \geq y$ and multiply the inequality by -2, the result is $-4x - 12 \leq -2y$.

INTERMEDIATE ALGEBRA

Intermediate algebra questions are some of the toughest questions on the ACT Math Test. To compensate for the difficulty of the topic, almost all of the intermediate algebra problems will be in basic form, meaning that you don't need to sort through a mess of words to find the question. Also, you should be glad to hear that there will be only nine intermediate algebra problems on the Math Test, making them worth less than one-sixth of your math score.

In this section, we'll present the intermediate algebra topics to you in the following order:

1. Solving and Factoring Quadratic Equations
2. Solving Systems of Equations
3. Relationships between the Sides of an Equation
4. Functions
5. Matrices
6. Logarithms

The first two topics in this list appear most frequently on the ACT. You may not encounter a single example of the last four topics, particularly the last two, on a given test. Those topics do appear from time to time, though, so it pays to be prepared for them.

Solving and Factoring Quadratic Equations

This topic constitutes a major portion of the intermediate algebra questions. You will probably see about three quadratic equations questions per test. Those three questions make up a third of the intermediate algebra questions. If you can master these questions, then you're well on your way to overcoming intermediate algebra.

Definition of a Quadratic Equation

A quadratic equation is a second-degree equation with one variable and usually two solutions. If you don't understand what that means, hold on a second. A quadratic equation on the ACT will almost always appear in the following form:

$$ax^2 + bx + c = 0$$

where a and b are coefficients and $a \neq 0$. That is the standard form of a quadratic equation, and it is the form that the ACT almost always uses. In some cases, you may come across an equation that looks like this:

$$ax^2 + c = bx$$

In this case you can subtract bx from both sides of the equation to get the equation into standard form:

$$ax^2 - bx + c = 0$$

Every quadratic equation contains a variable raised to the second power. In most of the quadratic equations you'll see on the test, there will be two solutions for this variable.

Also, the ACT almost always makes a equal to 1 to simplify solving these equations. (Note that when $a = 1x^2$, is simply written x^2.)

Solving a Quadratic Equation

Solving a quadratic equation means solving for the variable used in the equation. Almost all quadratic equations appearing on the ACT can be solved by factoring. Solving a quadratic equation by factoring is essentially the reverse of what you do when multiplying binomials. Take the following example:

$$x^2 + 9x + 18 = 0$$

Solving for x here requires a good degree of intuition, but with time and practice your intuition will become increasingly keen. Try to imagine which binomials would create the equation above. You can do this by considering the factors of 18 (1 and 18; 2 and 9; 3 and 6) and asking yourself which pair of factors adds up to 9. Done that? If so, you see that 3 and 6 add up to 9. So you can factor the equation as:

$$(x + 3)(x + 6) = 0$$

Whenever you see something in the above form, you can solve it like this:

$$x + 3 = 0 \qquad\qquad x + 6 = 0$$
$$x = -3 \qquad\qquad x = -6$$

Either $x = -3$ or $x = -6$ satisfies the equation.

The Quadratic Formula

Very rarely on the ACT, you may encounter a quadratic equation that cannot be solved by factoring. In that case, you can use the quadratic formula to solve the equation. The quadratic formula is:

$$x = \frac{-b \pm \sqrt{b^2 - 4ac}}{2a}$$

where a, b, and c are the same coefficients as in the quadratic equation. You simply plug in the coefficients to determine solutions for x. Just to prove to you that the equation works, we'll work out the quadratic equation whose roots we already know: $x^2 + 9x + 18 = 0$. Remember that it's in the form of $ax^2 + bx + c = 0$.

$$x = \frac{-9 \pm \sqrt{9^2 - 4 \times 1 \times 18}}{2 \times 1}$$
$$x = \frac{-9 \pm \sqrt{81 - 72}}{2}$$
$$x = \frac{-9 \pm \sqrt{9}}{2}$$
$$x = \frac{-9 \pm 3}{2}$$
$$x = \frac{-6}{2} = -3 \text{ or } x = \frac{-12}{2} = -6$$

Solving Systems of Equations

A few times per test, the ACT will give you two equations and ask you to determine the value of a particular variable or some other equation or expression. For example:

> If $3x + 4y = 32$ and $2y - x = 6$, then $x - y =$

The best way to answer this type of question is to use a substitution method: Solve for one variable and then substitute that value into the other equation. In looking at the two equations above, it seems obvious that it would be easier to solve for x using the second equation than it would be to solve for y in either of the two equations. All it takes is a little reorganizing:

$$2y - x = 6$$
$$2y - 6 = x$$
$$x = 2y - 6$$

Next, all we have to do is plug $2y - 6$ into the value for x in the first equation:

$$3(2y - 6) + 4y = 32$$

Now we have only one variable to deal with in the equation, and we can easily solve for it:

$$6y - 18 + 4y = 32$$
$$10y = 50$$
$$y = 5$$

Once we know the value of y, we can plug that value into either equation to solve for x:

$$x = 2y - 6$$
$$x = 2(5) - 6$$
$$x = 4$$

Now we can answer the question, which asked for $x - y$. We get $4 - 5 = -1$. When you solve systems of equations questions, always be careful of a few things:

1. When you first solve for one variable, make sure you solve for it in its lowest form (solve for x rather than $2x$).
2. When you substitute, make sure you correctly apply the distributive law of multiplication: $3(2y - 6) = 6y - 18$.
3. Always answer the question the ACT asks. For example, in the sample above, the question asked for the value of $x - y$. But it's certainly possible that after doing all the work and figuring out that $x = 4$ you might forget to carry out the final simple operation of $4 - 5 = -1$, and instead incorrectly answer 4.

Systems of Equations with Infinite Solutions

Occasionally, the ACT will test your understanding of systems of linear equations by asking you to determine when two equations in a system yield an infinite number of solutions. To answer this sort of question, you only need to know one thing: A system of equations will yield an infinite number of solutions when the two equations describe the same line. In other words, the system of equations will have an infinite number of solutions when the two equations are equal and in $y = mx + b$ form. Here's an example:

The following system of equations would have an infinite number of solutions for which of the following values of b?

$$3x - 2y = 4$$
$$12x - 4by = 16$$

A. 1
B. 2
C. 4
D. 8
E. 12

To answer this question, you have to pick a value for b such that the two equations have the same formula fitting the $y = mx + b$ form. The first step in this process is to transfer $3x - 2y = 4$ into the $y = mx + b$ form:

$$3x - 2y = 4$$
$$-2y = -3x + 4$$
$$y = \frac{3}{2}x - 2$$

Then put $12x - 4by = 16$ into the same form:

$$12x - 4by = 16$$
$$-4by = -12x + 16$$
$$by = 3x - 4$$
$$y = \frac{3x}{b} - \frac{4}{b}$$

Since you know that the two equations have to be equal, you know that $\frac{3}{2}x$ must equal $\frac{3x}{b}$. This means that $b = 2$, so **B** is the right answer to the question.

Relationships between the Sides of an Equation

You should understand the relationship between the two sides of an equation. If you have an equation that says $w = kt^2$, where k is a constant, the equation tells you that w varies directly with the square of t; in other words, as t increases, so does w.

If, on the other hand, you have an equation that says $w = k/t^2$, where k is a constant, the equation tells you that w varies inversely with the square of t; in other words, as t increases, w decreases.

Functions

If you restated $y = ax + b$ as $f(x) = ax + b$, you would have a function, $f(x)$, which is pronounced "f of x." On the ACT, you can almost always treat $f(x)$ as you would treat y, but we want you to be aware of the different format.

Compound Functions

On rare occasions, the ACT has asked questions about compound functions, in which one function is worked out in terms of another. The notation for a compound function is $f(g(x))$, or $f \circ g$. To evaluate a compound function like $f(g(x))$, first evaluate g at x. Then evaluate f at the results of $g(x)$. Basically, work with the inner parentheses first, and then the outer ones, just like in any other algebraic expression. Try the following example:

Suppose $h(x) = x2 + 2x$ and $j(x) = \left| \dfrac{x}{4} + 2 \right|$. What is $j(h(4))$?

$$(j \circ h)(4) = j(h(4))$$
$$= j(4^2 + 2(4))$$
$$= j(16 + 8)$$
$$= \left| \frac{24}{4} + 2 \right|$$
$$= |8|$$
$$= 8$$

Here's a slightly more complicated example:

Suppose $f(x) = 3x + 1$ and $g(x) = \sqrt{5x}$. What is $g(f(x))$?

This question doesn't ask you to evaluate the compound function for a given value—it asks you to express the compound function as a single function. To do so, simply plug the formula for f into the formula for g:

$$g(f(x)) = g(3x+1)$$
$$g(f(x)) = \sqrt{5(3x+1)}$$
$$g(f(x)) = \sqrt{15x+5s}$$

Matrices

You will seldom see a matrix problem on the ACT, and many high school math courses may not have covered matrices by the time you take the test. Still, any matrix problems on the ACT will be very straightforward and fundamental, so you really only need to know the basics of matrices in order to get the right answers. We will cover those basics here.

Adding and Subtracting Matrices

You will not be asked to do anything more advanced than adding or subtracting matrices. For example,

$$A = \begin{bmatrix} 2 & 0 \\ 3 & -5 \end{bmatrix} \quad B = \begin{bmatrix} -4 & 1 \\ 6 & 3 \end{bmatrix}$$

What is $A + B$? To answer this question, you simply add the corresponding entries in A and B. The entries in the first row are $2 + (-4) = -2$ and $0 + 1 = 1$. The entries in the second row are $3 + 6 = 9$ and $(-5) + 3 = -2$. So the resulting matrix is:

$$A + B = \begin{bmatrix} -2 & 1 \\ 9 & -2 \end{bmatrix}$$

If the question had asked you what $A - B$ is, then you would simply subtract the entries in B from the corresponding entries in A.

Logarithms

Like matrices, logarithms rarely appear in the ACT Math Test. But they do pop up occasionally, and you should know how to handle them. Logarithmic functions are inverses of exponential functions. The exponential equation $x = a^b$ is equivalent to the logarithmic equation $\log_a x = b$.

This inverse relationship between logs and exponents is all you need to know in order to answer a logarithm question on the ACT. If you see $\log_x 16 = 4$, then you know that $x^4 = 16$. You will be able to use this second, more manageable mathematical expression to answer the question.

COORDINATE GEOMETRY

Coordinate geometry is geometry dealing primarily with the line graphs and the (x,y) coordinate plane. The ACT Math Test includes nine questions on coordinate geometry. The topics you need to know are:

1. Number Lines and Inequalities
2. The (x,y) Coordinate Plane
3. Distance and Midpoints
4. Slope
5. Parallel and Perpendicular Lines
6. The Equation of a Line
7. Graphing Equations
8. Conic Sections

Most of the questions on coordinate geometry focus on slope. About two questions on each test will cover number lines and inequalities. The other topics are usually covered by just one question, if they are covered at all.

Number Lines and Inequalities

Number line questions generally ask you to graph inequalities. A typical number line graph question will ask you:

What is the graph of the solution set for $2(x + 5) > 4$?

To answer this question, you first must solve for x.

1. Divide both sides by 2 to get: $x + 5 > 2$
2. Subtract 5 from both sides to get: $x > -3$

Now you match $x > -3$ to its line graph:

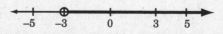

The circles at the endpoints of a line indicating an inequality are very important when trying to match an inequality to a line graph. An open circle at -3 denotes that x is greater than but *not* equal to -3. A closed circle would have indicated that x is greater than *or* equal to -3.

For the solution set $-3 < x < 3$, where x must be greater than -3 and less than 3, the line graph looks like this:

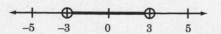

The (x,y) Coordinate Plane

The (x,y) coordinate plane is described by two perpendicular lines, the x-axis and the y-axis. The intersection of these axes is called the origin. The location of any other point on the plane (which extends in all directions without limit) can be described by a pair of coordinates. Here is a figure of the coordinate plane with a few points drawn in and labeled with their coordinates:

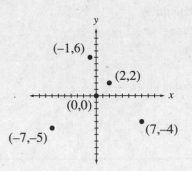

As you can see from the figure, each of the points on the coordinate plane receives a pair of coordinates: (x,y). The first coordinate in a coordinate pair is called the x-coordinate. The x-coordinate of a point is its location along the x-axis and can be determined by the point's distance from the y-axis ($x = 0$ at the y-axis). If the point is to the right of the y-axis, its x-coordinate is positive; if the point is to the left of the y-axis, its x-coordinate is negative.

The second coordinate in a coordinate pair is the y-coordinate. The y-coordinate of a point is its location along the y-axis and can be calculated as the distance from that point to the x-axis. If the point is above the x-axis, its y-coordinate is positive; if the point is below the x-axis, its y-coordinate is negative.

The ACT often tests your understanding of the coordinate plane and coordinates by telling you the coordinates of the vertices of a defined geometric shape like a square and then asking you to pick the coordinates of the last vertex. For example:

> In the standard (x,y) coordinate plane, 3 corners of a square are $(2,-2)$, $(-2,-2)$, and $(-2,2)$. What are the coordinates of the square's fourth corner?

The best way to solve this sort of problem is to draw a quick sketch of the coordinate plane and the coordinates given. You'll then be able to see the shape described and pick out the coordinates of the final vertex from the image. In this case, the sketch would look like this:

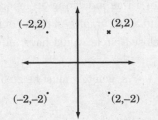

A square is the easiest geometric shape that a question might concern. It is possible that you will be asked to deal with rectangles or right triangles. The method for any geometric shape is the same, though. Sketch it out so you can see it.

Distance

The ACT occasionally asks test-takers to measure the distance between two points on the coordinate plane. Luckily, measuring distance in the coordinate plane is made easy thanks to the Pythagorean theorem. If you are given two points, (x_2, y_1) and (x_2, y_2), their distance will always be given by the following formula:

$$\text{Distance} = \sqrt{(x_2 - x_1)^2 + (y_2 - y_1)^2}$$

The distance between two points can be represented by the hypotenuse of a right triangle whose legs are of lengths $(x_2 - x_1)$ and $(y_2 - y_1)$. The following diagram shows how the formula is based on the Pythagorean theorem (see p. 65).

$$d = \sqrt{(x_2 - x_1)^2 + (y_2 - y_1)^2}$$

Here's a sample problem:

Calculate the distance between (4,–3) and (–3,8).

To solve this problem, just plug the proper numbers into the distance formula:

$$\text{Distance} = \sqrt{((-3) - 4)^2 + (8 - (-3))^2} = \sqrt{49 + 121} = \sqrt{170}$$

The distance between the points is $\sqrt{170}$, which equals approximately 13.04.

Finding Midpoints

Like finding the distance between two points, the midpoint between two points in the coordinate plane can be calculated using a formula. If the endpoints of a line segment are (x_1, y_1) and (x_2, y_2), then the midpoint of the line segment is:

$$\text{Midpoint} = \left(\frac{x_1 + x_2}{2}, \frac{y_1 + y_2}{2} \right)$$

In other words, the x- and y-coordinates of the midpoint are the averages of the x- and y-coordinates of the endpoints.

Here is a practice question:

What is the midpoint of the line segment whose endpoints are (6, 0) and (3, 7)?

All you have to do is plug the end points into the midpoint formula. According to the question, $x_1 = 6$, $y_1 = 0$, $x_2 = 3$, and $y_2 = 7$:

$$\text{Midpoint} = \left(\frac{6=3}{2}, \frac{0+7}{2} \right) = \left(\frac{9}{2}, \frac{7}{2} \right) = (4.5, 3.5)$$

Slope

The slope of a line is a measurement of how steeply the line climbs or falls as it moves from left to right. More technically, the slope is a line's vertical change divided by its horizontal change, also known as "rise over run." Given two points on a line, (x_1, y_1) and (x_2, y_2), the slope of that line can be calculated using the following formula:

$$\text{Slope} = \frac{y_2 - y_1}{x_2 - x_1}$$

The variable most often used to represent slope is m.

So, for example, the slope of a line that contains the points (–2, –4) and (6, 1) is:

$$m = \frac{1 - (-4)}{6 - (-2)} = \frac{5}{8}$$

Positive and Negative Slopes

You can easily determine whether the slope of a line is positive or negative just by looking at the line. If a line slopes uphill as you trace it from left to right, the slope is positive. If a line slopes downhill as you trace it from left to right, the slope is negative.

You can determine the relative magnitude of the slope by the steepness of the line. The steeper the line, the more the "rise" will exceed the "run," and the larger $y_2 - y_1$ and, consequently, the slope will be. Conversely, the flatter the line, the smaller the slope will be.

For practice, look at the lines in the figure below and try to determine whether their slopes are positive or negative and which have greater relative slopes:

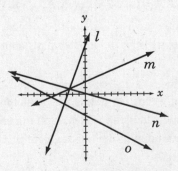

Lines l and m have positive slopes, and lines n and o have negative slopes. In terms of slope magnitude, line $l > m > n > o$.

Special Slopes

It can be helpful to recognize a few slopes by sight.

- A line that is horizontal has a slope of 0. Since there is no "rise," $y_2 - y_1 = 0$, and thus $m = (y_2 - y_1)/(x_2 - x_1) = 0/(x_2 - x_1) = 0$.
- A line that is vertical has an undefined slope. In this case, there is no "run," and $x_2 - x_1 = 0$. Thus $m = (y_2 - y_1)/(x_2 - x_1) = ((y_2 - y_1)/0)$, and any fraction with 0 in its denominator is, by definition, undefined.
- A line that makes a 45° angle with a horizontal has a slope of 1 or –1. This makes sense because the "rise" equals the "run," and $y_2 - y_1 = x_2 - x_1$ or $y_2 - y_1 = -(x_2 - x_1)$.

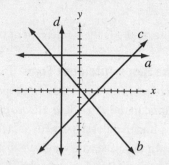

Line *a* has slope 0 because it is horizontal. Line *b* has slope –1 because it makes a 45° angle with the horizontal and slopes downward as you move from left to right. Line *c* has slope 1 because it makes a 45° angle with the horizontal and slopes upward as you move from left to right. Line *d* has undefined slope because it is vertical.

Parallel and Perpendicular Lines

Parallel lines are lines that don't intersect. In other words, parallel lines are lines that share the exact same slope.

Perpendicular lines are lines that intersect at a right angle (or 90°). In coordinate geometry, perpendicular lines have negative reciprocal slopes. That is, a line with slope m is perpendicular to a line with a slope of $\dfrac{-1}{m}$.

In the figure below are three lines. Lines *q* and *r* both have a slope of 2, so they are parallel. Line *s* is perpendicular to both lines *q* and *r*, and thus has a slope of $\dfrac{-1}{2}$.

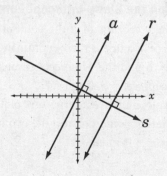

On the ACT, never assume that two lines are parallel or perpendicular just because they look that way in a diagram. If the lines are parallel or perpendicular, the ACT will tell you so. (Perpendicular lines can be indicated by a little square located at the place of intersection, as in the diagram above.)

Equation of a Line

We've already shown you how to find the slope of a line using two points on the line. It is also possible to find the slope of a line using the equation of the line. In addition, the equation of a line can help you find the *x*- and *y*-intercepts of the line, which are the locations where the line intersects with the *x*- and *y*-axes. This equation for a line is called the slope-intercept form:

$$y = mx + b$$

where *m* is the slope of the line, and *b* is the *y*-intercept of the line.

Finding the Slope Using the Slope-Intercept Form

If you are given the equation of a line that matches the slope-intercept form, you immediately know that the slope is equal to the value of *m*. However, it is more likely that the ACT will give you an equation for a line that doesn't exactly match the slope-intercept form and ask you to calculate the slope. In this case, you will have to manipulate the given equation until it resembles the slope-intercept form. For example:

What is the slope of the line defined by the equation 5x + 3y = 6?

To answer this question, isolate the *y* so that the equation fits the slope-intercept form.

$$5x + 3y = 6$$
$$3y = -5x + 6$$
$$y = -\frac{5}{3}x + 2$$

The slope of the line is $\frac{-5}{3}$.

Finding the Intercepts Using the Slope-Intercept Form

The *y*-intercept of a line is the *y*-coordinate of the point at which the line intersects the *y*-axis. Likewise, the *x*-intercept of a line is the *x*-coordinate of the point at which the line intersects the *x*-axis. In order to find the *y*-intercept, simply set *x* = 0 and solve for the value of *y*. To find the *x*-intercept, set *y* = 0 and solve for *x*.

To sketch a line given in slope-intercept form, first plot the *y*-intercept, and then use the slope of the line to plot another point. Connect the two points to form your line. In the figure below, the line *y* = –2*x* + 3 is graphed.

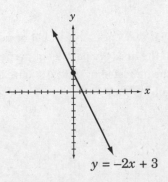

$$y = -2x + 3$$

Since the slope is equal to –2, the line descends two units for every one unit it moves in the positive x direction. The y-intercept is at 3, so the line crosses the y-axis at $(0,3)$.

Graphing Equations

For the ACT Math Test, you should know how the graphs of certain equations look. The two equations that are most important in terms of graphing are $y = x^2$ and $y = x^3$.

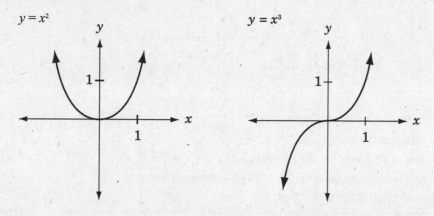

If you add lesser-degree terms to the equations, these graphs will shift around the origin but retain their basic shape. You should also keep in mind what the negatives of these equations look like:

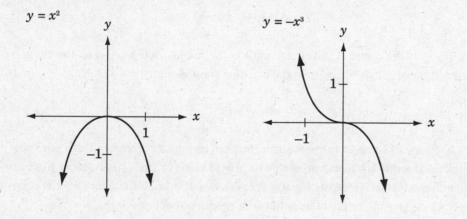

Conic Sections

Occasionally, the ACT will test your knowledge of parabolas, circles, or ellipses. These topics do not regularly appear on the ACT, but it still pays to prepare: If these topics do appear, getting them right can separate you from the crowd.

Parabolas

A parabola is a "U"-shaped curve that can open either upward or downward.

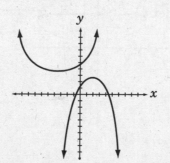

A parabola is the graph of a quadratic function, which, you may recall, follows the form $ax^2 + bx + c$. The equation of a parabola gives you quite a bit of information about the parabola.

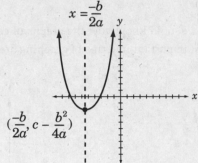

1. The vertex of the parabola is $(\frac{-b}{2a}, c - \frac{b^2}{4a})$.
2. The axis of symmetry of the parabola is the line $x = \frac{-b}{2a}$.
3. The parabola opens upward if $a > 0$ and downward if $a < 0$.
4. The y-intercept is the point $(0,c)$.

Circles

A circle is the collection of points equidistant from a given point, called the center of the circle. Circles are defined by the formula:

$$(x - h)^2 + (y - k)^2 = r^2$$

where (h, k) is the center of the circle, and r is the radius. Note that when the circle is centered at the origin, $h = k = 0$, so the equation simplifies to:

$$x^2 + y^2 = r^2$$

That's it. That's all you need to know about circles in coordinate geometry. Once you know and understand this equation, you should be able to sketch a circle in its proper place on the coordinate system if given its equation. You should also be able to figure out the equation of a circle given a picture of its graph with coordinates labeled.

Ellipses

An ellipse is a figure shaped like an oval. It looks like a circle somebody sat on, but it is actually a good deal more complicated than a circle, as you can see from all the jargon on the diagram below.

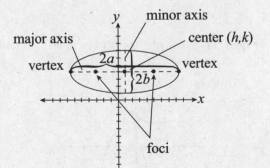

The two foci are crucial to the definition of an ellipse. The sum of the distances from the foci to any point on the ellipse is constant. To understand this visually, look at the figure below. The quantity $d1 + d2$ is constant for each point on the ellipse.

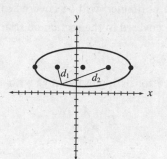

The line segment containing the foci of an ellipse with both endpoints on the ellipse is called the major axis. The endpoints of the major axis are called the vertices. The line segment perpendicularly bisecting the major axis with both endpoints on the ellipse is the minor axis. The point midway between the foci is the center of the ellipse. When you see an ellipse, you should be able to identify where each of these components would be.

The equation of an ellipse is:

$$\frac{(x-h)^2}{a^2}+\frac{(y-k)^2}{b^2}=1$$

where a, b, h, and k are constants. With respect to this formula, remember that:

1. The center of the ellipse is (h,k).
2. The length of the horizontal axis is $2a$.
3. The length of the vertical axis is $2b$.
4. If $a > b$, the major axis is horizontal and the minor axis is vertical; if $b > a$, the major axis is vertical and the minor axis is horizontal.

PLANE GEOMETRY

Plane geometry problems account for 14 questions on the ACT Math Test—that's almost a quarter of the questions on the subject test. If you've taken high school geometry, you've probably covered all of the topics reviewed here. If you haven't taken high school geometry, you should consider taking the ACT after you've taken a geometry course, or, if that's not possible, enlisting the help of a geometry teacher. While you can probably get by on the ACT without knowing trigonometry or intermediate algebra very well, you cannot get by without a solid understanding of plane geometry because these questions constitute such a significant part of the test.

In this section, we'll cover these plane geometry topics in the following order:

1. Angles and Lines
2. Triangles
3. Polygons

4. Circles

5. Simple Three-Dimensional Geometry

Key topics, such as area and perimeter, will be covered in the relevant sections. For instance, areas of triangles are covered in the section on triangles.

Angles and Lines

An angle is a geometric figure consisting of two rays with a common endpoint:

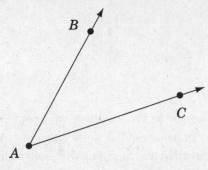

The common endpoint of the rays is called the vertex of the angle. In this case, the vertex is point A, which is a part of the ray $\overrightarrow{AB}$ as well as the ray $\overrightarrow{AC}$. The angle can be called either $\angle CAB$ or $\angle BAC$. The only rule in naming an angle is that the vertex must always be the middle "initial" of the angle.

Measuring Angles

Angles are measured in degrees, sometimes denoted by the symbol °. There are 360° in a complete rotation around a point; a circle therefore has 360 degrees.

Consider two intersecting lines. The intersection of these lines produces four angles:

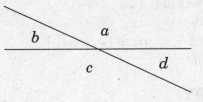

From the diagram below, you should see that the four angles together encompass one full revolution around the two lines' point of intersection. Therefore, the four angles produced by two intersection lines total 360 degrees; angles $a + b + c + d = 360°$.

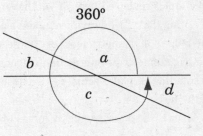

Types of Angles

There are many different types of angles, all categorized by the number of degrees they have.

Acute and Obtuse Angles

As shown in the diagram below, an acute angle is an angle that is smaller than 90°, while an obtuse angle is an angle that is greater than 90° but less than 180°.

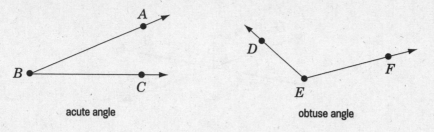

acute angle   obtuse angle

Right Angles

An angle with a measure of 90° is called a right angle. Notice that a right angle is symbolized by a square drawn in the corner of the angle. Whenever you see that little square, you know that you are dealing with a right angle. You also know that the lines that meet at the right angle are perpendicular.

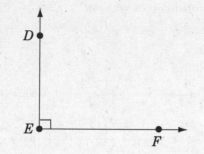

Complementary and Supplementary Angles

Special names are given to pairs of angles whose sums equal either 90° or 180°. Two angles whose sum is 90° are called complementary angles. If two angles add up to 180°, they are called supplementary angles.

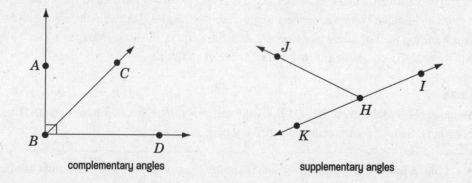

complementary angles   supplementary angles

Angles *ABC* and *CBD* are complementary, whereas angles *KHJ* and *JHI* are supplementary.

It is important to remember that these terms are only relative. An angle is only supplementary or complementary to *another specific angle*. A single angle, when considered alone, can be neither supplementary nor complementary—it can only take on one of these properties when considered as part of a pair of angles.

Vertical Angles

When two lines (or segments) intersect, the angles that lie opposite each other, called vertical angles, are always equal.

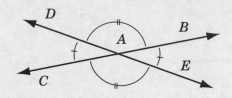

Angles *DAC* and *BAE* are vertical angles and are therefore equal to each other. Angles *DAB* and *CAE* are also vertical (and equal) angles.

Parallel Lines Cut by a Transversal

Occasionally on the ACT, you will run into a problem in which two parallel lines are cut by a third straight line, known as a transversal. The eight angles created by these two intersections have special relationships with one another.

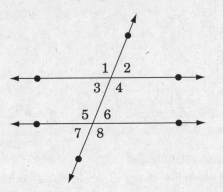

Angles 1, 4, 5, and 8 are all equal to each other. So are angles 2, 3, 6, and 7. Also, the sum of any two adjacent angles, such as 1 and 2 or 6 and 8, equals 180°. From these rules, you can make justified claims about seemingly unrelated angles. For example, since angles 1 and 2 add up to 180°, and since angles 2 and 7 are equal, the sum of angles 1 and 7 also equals 180°, based on the substitution principle of addition.

Lines

You may see a problem on the ACT that asks you about lines. In order to understand these questions, there is some vocabulary that you need to know.

- **Line.** A line is a set of infinite points that runs straight. If you have two points, the line will run straight through them and extend infinitely in both directions.

- **Line Segment.** A line segment consists of two points (endpoints) and all the points on a straight line between them. If you have a line segment that stretches from point A to point B, the line segment will be referred to as $\overline{AB}$.

$$\underset{A \qquad\qquad B}{\bullet\!\!\rule[0.4ex]{3cm}{0.4pt}\!\!\bullet}$$

- **Ray.** A ray is a line that has one endpoint; it extends infinitely in the direction without the endpoint.

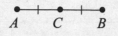

- **Midpoint.** A midpoint is the point exactly halfway between the two endpoints of a line segment.

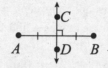

- **Bisect (verb).** Anything that bisects a line segment cuts the line segment exactly in half, at the midpoint. Line $\overline{CD}$ bisects line segment $\overline{AB}$.

And that's all the line vocab you need for the ACT Math Test.

Triangles

On each ACT Math Test, you will see three or four questions on triangles. These questions tend to deal with the angles and sides of triangles, but you may also see questions about their areas and perimeters.

Triangles are closed figures containing three angles and three sides. There are a number of important rules about these angles and sides that, if mastered, will take you a long way on the ACT.

- The sum of the three angles in a triangle will always equal 180°. Thus, if you know the measure of two angles in a triangle, you can calculate the measure of the third angle.
- The exterior angle of a triangle is always equal to the sum of the remote interior angles (i.e., the angles that are not adjacent to the exterior angle). In the figure, the exterior angle, x, is equal to 140°, which is the sum of the two remote interior angles.

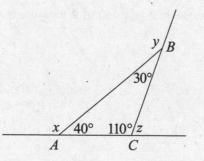

- The sum of the exterior angles of a triangle will always equal 360°, therefore

$$\angle x + \angle y + \angle z = 360°.$$

- The longest side of a triangle is always opposite the largest angle; the second-longest side is opposite the second-largest angle; the shortest side is opposite the smallest angle. Therefore, in the triangle above, $\angle ACB$ is the largest angle, so its opposite side, $\overline{AB}$, is the longest side. No side of a triangle can be as long as the sum of the other two side lengths. Therefore, in the triangle above, $\overline{AB} < \overline{BC} + \overline{CA}$.

- If you know that a triangle has sides of length 4 and 6, you know the third side is shorter than 10 and longer than 2. This can help you eliminate possible answer choices on multiple-choice questions.

There are a number of specialized types of triangles. We'll discuss them below.

Isosceles Triangles

Isosceles triangles have two equal sides, in this case sides a and b (the little marks on those two sides mean that the sides are congruent, which means equal). The angles opposite the congruent sides, in this case angles A and B, are also equal.

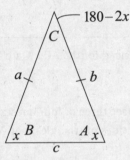

Because these two angles are equal, and the sum of a triangle's angles is always 180°, if you know the value of one of the two equal angles, let's say angle A, you know the value of all the angles in the triangle. Angle B is equal to A. Angle C is equal to $180 - 2A$ (since A and B are equal, $A + B = 2A$). The same is true if you start with the measure of angle C: Angles A and B each measure $\dfrac{(180 - C)}{2}$.

Equilateral Triangles

An equilateral triangle is a triangle in which all the sides and all the angles are equal. Since the angles of a triangle must total 180°, the measure of each angle of an equilateral triangle must be 60°.

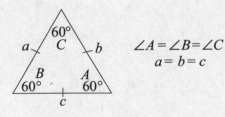

Right Triangles

A triangle with a right angle (90°) is called a right triangle. Because the angles of a triangle must total 180°, the nonright angles (angles A and B in the diagram below) in a right triangle must add up to 90° (that is, they are complementary). The side opposite the right angle (side c in the diagram below) is called the hypotenuse.

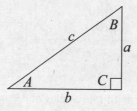

The Pythagorean Theorem

The Pythagorean theorem defines the relationship between the sides of every right triangle. The theorem states that the length of the hypotenuse squared is equal to the sum of the squares of the lengths of the legs:

$$c^2 = a^2 + b^2$$

If you are given any two sides of a right triangle, you can use the Pythagorean theorem to calculate the length of the third side.

Certain groups of three integers can be the lengths of a right triangle. Such groups of integers are called Pythagorean triples. Some common Pythagorean triples include {3, 4, 5}, {5, 12, 13}, {8, 15, 17}, {7, 24, 25}, and {9, 40, 41}. Any multiple of one of these groups is also a Pythagorean triple. For example, {9, 12, 15} = 3{3, 4, 5}. If you know these basic Pythagorean triples, they can help you quickly determine, without calculation, the length of a side of a right triangle in a problem that gives you the length of the other two sides.

Special Right Triangles

There are two kinds of special right triangles for which you don't have to use the Pythagorean theorem because their sides always exist in the same distinct ratios. This is not to say that you *can't* use the Pythagorean theorem when dealing with these triangles, just that you don't have to, since you can work out problems very quickly if you know the ratios. The two types of triangles are called 30-60-90 and 45-45-90 right triangles.

A 30-60-90 triangle is, as you may have guessed, a triangle with angles of 30°, 60°, and 90°. What makes it special is the specific pattern that the side-length of 30-60-90 triangles follow. Suppose the short leg, opposite the 30° angle, has length x. Then the hypotenuse has length $2x$, and the long leg, opposite the 60° angle, has length $x\sqrt{3}$. Study the following diagram, which shows these ratios:

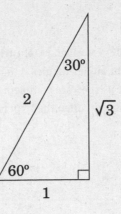

A 45-45-90 triangle is a triangle with two angles of 45° and one right angle. This type of triangle is also known as an isosceles right triangle, since it's both isosceles and right. Like the 30-60-90 triangle, the lengths of the sides of a 45-45-90 triangle also follow a specific pattern that you should know. If the legs are of length x (they are always equal), then the hypotenuse has length $x\sqrt{2}$. Take a look at this diagram:

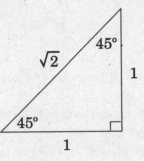

Similarity in Triangles

In reference to triangles, the word similar means "shaped in the same way." Two triangles are similar if their corresponding angles are equal. If this is the case, then the lengths of corresponding sides will be proportional to each other. For example, if triangles ABC and DEF are similar, then sides $\overline{AB}$ and $\overline{DE}$ correspond to each other, as do $\overline{BC}$ and $\overline{EF}$, and $\overline{CA}$ and $\overline{FD}$.

The proportionality of corresponding sides means that:

$$\frac{AB}{DE} = \frac{BC}{EF} = \frac{CA}{FD}$$

The properties of similarity will almost definitely be tested on the ACT. Let's say you come across the following question:

Triangles ABC and DEC are similar, and line l is parallel to segment $\overline{AB}$. What is the length of $\overline{CE}$?

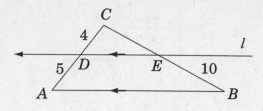

If you know the rule of similarity, you will quickly realize that the ratio $\overline{CD}:\overline{CA}$ is 4:9 and that $\overline{CE}:\overline{CB}$ must have the same ratio. Since $\overline{EB}$ is equal to 10, the only possible length of $\overline{CE}$ is 8, since 8:18 is equivalent to 4:9.

Two triangles are similar if they have two pairs of corresponding angles and one pair of sides that are equal, or if one pair of angles is equal and the two pairs of adjacent sides are proportional.

Area of a Triangle

The area of a triangle is equal to one-half the base of the triangle times the height, or $\left(\dfrac{1}{2}\right)bh$. For example, given the following triangle,

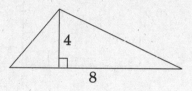

the area equals $\left(\dfrac{1}{2}\right)(4\times8)=16$. If you know the length of one leg of a triangle and can determine the height of the triangle (using that leg as a base), then you can plug those two numbers into the area formula.

Perimeter of a Triangle

The perimeter of a triangle is equal to the sum of the lengths of the triangle's three sides. If a triangle has sides of length 4, 6, and 9, then its perimeter is 4 + 6 + 9 = 19.

Polygons

Polygon questions on the Math Test tend to deal with perimeters and areas, so you should pay particular attention to those sections below.

By definition, a polygon is a two-dimensional figure with three or more straight sides. Under that definition, triangles are a type of polygon. However, since triangles are such an important part of the ACT, we gave them their own section. This section will deal with polygons of four sides or more.

Perimeter of Polygons

As with triangles, the perimeter of a polygon is equal to the sum of the lengths of its sides. Perimeter problems on the ACT usually involve unconventional polygons like this one:

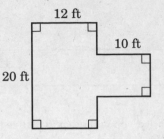

If you saw this polygon on the ACT, you would probably be asked to determine its perimeter. These questions can be tricky because of the number of sides involved and the number of sides the ACT decides to label. Wouldn't it have been easier if all the sides were labeled? Yes, it would have been easier, which is why the ACT didn't label them. Still, if you think about it, this question isn't hard. In fact, if you flipped the lines out in the upper-right and lower-right corners, you would have a rectangle:

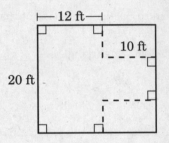

The ACT writers were kind enough to give you the height of the rectangle (20 ft), and you can figure out the width of the rectangle by adding 12 ft and 10 ft to get 22 ft. So the perimeter of this normal rectangle masquerading as a weird polygon is $2l + 2w$ or $2 \times 20 + 2 \times 22 = 84$ ft.

Parallelograms

A parallelogram is a quadrilateral whose opposite sides are parallel.

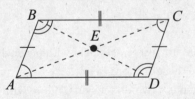

In a parallelogram:

1. Opposite sides are equal in length; $\overline{BC} = \overline{AD}$ and $\overline{BA} = \overline{CD}$.
2. Opposite angles are equal; $\angle A = \angle C$; $\angle B = \angle D$.
3. Adjacent angles are supplementary.
4. The diagonals bisect each other; therefore, $\overline{BE} = \overline{ED}$ and $\overline{AE} = \overline{EC}$.
5. Each diagonal splits a parallelogram into two congruent triangles; $\triangle ACD \cong \triangle ABC$.
6. Two diagonals split a parallelogram into two pairs of congruent triangles; $\triangle ABE \cong \triangle DEC$ and $\triangle BEC \cong \triangle AED$.

Area of a Parallelogram

To calculate the area of a parallelogram, we must introduce a new term: altitude. The altitude of a parallelogram is the line segment perpendicular to a pair of opposite sides with one endpoint on each side. Below are various parallelograms and their altitudes.

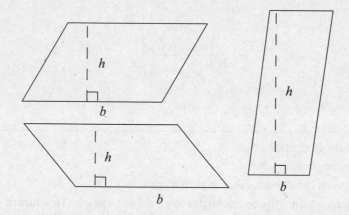

The area of a parallelogram is the product of the length of its altitude and the length of a side that contains an endpoint of the altitude. This side is called the base of the parallelogram. Any side can become a base of a given parallelogram: All you need to do is draw an altitude from it to the opposite side. A common way to describe the area of a parallelogram is the base times the height, where the height is the altitude:

$$A = b \times h$$

Rectangles

A rectangle is a specialized parallelogram whose angles all equal 90°. All the rules that hold for parallelograms hold for rectangles. A rectangle has further properties, however:

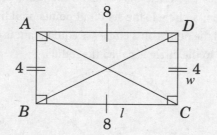

In a rectangle:

---

1. The angles are all equal to 90°.
2. The diagonals are equal in length; $\overline{BD} = \overline{AC}$.

Area of a Rectangle

The area of a rectangle is equal to its length multiplied by its width:

$$A = lw$$

In the case of the rectangle pictured above, the area equals $4 \times 8 = 32$ square units.

Squares

A square is a specific kind of rectangle where all of the sides are of equal length.

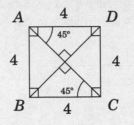

In a square:

1. All sides are of equal length.
2. All angles are equal to 90°.
3. The diagonals bisect each other at right angles; $\overline{BD} \perp \overline{AC}$.
4. The diagonals bisect the vertex angles to create 45° angles. (This means that the two diagonals break the square into four 45-45-90 triangles.)
5. The diagonals are equal in length; $\overline{BD} = \overline{AC}$.

Area of a Square

The area of a square is equal to the square of the length of a side:

$$A = s^2$$

In the case of the square above, the area is 16. Notice that the calculation for a square's area is essentially the same calculation as that of a rectangle's area (length times width).

Circles

You may encounter one or two circle questions on the Math Test. As we said in the co-ordinate geometry section, a circle is the set of all points equidistant from a given point. The point from which all the points on a circle are equidistant is called the center, and the distance from that point to the circle is called the radius.

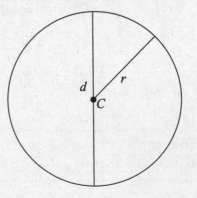

The circle above has its center at point C and a radius of length r. All circles also have a diameter, d. The diameter of a circle is a line segment that contains the center and whose endpoints are both on the circle. The length of the diameter is twice that of the radius.

Circumference of a Circle

The formula to find the circumference of a circle is:

$$C = 2\pi r$$

where r stands for the length of the radius. Because two times the radius is also equal to a circle's diameter, the formula for the circumference of a circle can also be written as πd.

Area of a Circle

The area of a circle is the radius squared multiplied by π:

$$A = \pi r^2$$

Simple Three-Dimensional Geometry

Solids are three-dimensional shapes. You probably will not see any questions on solids on the Math Test. When these questions do show up, they almost always cover rectangular solids, which are the easiest solids with which to work.

A rectangular solid is a six-faced, three-dimensional shape with six rectangular faces.

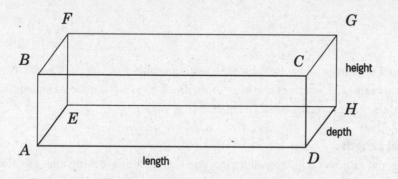

Just as squares are specialized rectangles, cubes are specialized rectangular solids. For a cube, the length, width, and height are all equal.

Surface Area

The surface area of a solid is the area of its outermost skin. A cardboard box, for example, is made up of a bunch of rectangles fastened together. The sum of the areas of those rectangles is the surface area of the cardboard box.

To calculate the surface area of a rectangular solid, all you have to do is find the area of each of the sides and add them. In fact, your job is even easier than that. The six sides of a rectangular solid can be divided into three pairs of two. If you look at the solid diagrammed above, you should see that panel *ABFE* = *DCGH*, *BCDA* = *FGHE*, and *BCGF* = *ADHE*. Therefore, you only have to calculate the areas of one of each of the three pairs, add those areas, and multiply that answer by two.

With a cube, finding the surface area is even easier. By definition, each side of a cube will always be the same, so to calculate the surface area, find the area of one side and multiply by six.

There is one property of surface area of which you should be aware. Imagine a rectangular solid that has a length of 8, a width of 4, and a height of 4. Now imagine a giant cleaver that comes and cuts the solid into two cubes, each of which has a length, width, and height of 4. Do the two cubes have a bigger combined surface area, a smaller combined surface area, or a combined surface area equal to the original solid? The answer is that the two cubes have a bigger surface area. Think about the cleaver coming down: It cuts the original solid in half, meaning it creates two new faces that are now on the surface. Whenever something is cut in half, or in pieces, its surface area increases (although its volume is unchanged).

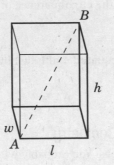

Volume

The volume of a rectangular solid can be found by multiplying the length by the width by the height. In other words:

$$V = lwh$$

Because all the dimensions of a cube are equal, the volume of a cube is even easier to calculate: Just raise the length of one edge to the third power. If a cube has a length, width, and height of 3, the volume equals $3^3 = 27$.

Diagonal Length

The diagonal of a rectangular solid is the line segment whose endpoints are at opposite corners. Each rectangular solid has four diagonals, all with the same length, which connect each pair of opposite vertices.

The formula for the length of a diagonal is:

$$d = \sqrt{l^2 + w^2 + h^2}$$

where l is the length, w is the width, and h is the height.

You can think of this formula as the Pythagorean theorem in three dimensions. In fact, you can derive this formula using the Pythagorean theorem. First, find the length of the diagonal along the base. This is $\sqrt{l^2 + w^2}$. Then use the Pythagorean theorem again, incorporating height to find the length of the diagonal from one corner to the other: $d^2 = \left(\sqrt{l^2 + w^2}\right)^2 + h^2$. Thus $d^2 = l^2 + w^2 + h^2$ and $d = \sqrt{l^2 + w^2 + h^2}$.

TRIGONOMETRY

At last we've arrived at everyone's favorite part of the Math Test. At least, it's our favorite. We're not sure what all the fuss is about when it comes to ACT trig. Many students are a little scared of trig, but the ACT seems to overcompensate for that fact by testing trig in an extremely straightforward way. ACT trig is basically all about right triangles. If you felt comfortable in the triangle section, trig will be a breeze. If you didn't feel too comfortable, learning a bit of trig can help you. When it comes down to it, you only have to be comfortable with the most basic aspects of trig to do well on the ACT trig questions.

Finally, there will only be four trig questions on the Math Test, so even if you aren't comfortable with trig, it won't destroy your Math score. The topics of trigonometry covered by the ACT are:

1. SOHCAHTOA
2. Solving Triangles
3. Trigonometric Identities
4. Trigonometric Graphs

SOHCAHTOA: Sine, Cosine, and Tangent

If you can remember the acronym SOHCAHTOA, you'll do really well on the trig questions. Yup, it's as easy as that. This acronym captures almost everything you'll need to know to answer ACT trig questions. It means:

SOH: **S**ine (**O**pposite over **H**ypotenuse)

CAH: **C**osine (**A**djacent over **H**ypotenuse)

TOA: **T**angent (**O**pposite over **A**djacent)

All of this opposite-adjacent-hypotenuse business in the parentheses tells you how to calculate the sine, cosine, and tangent of a right triangle. Opposite means the side facing the angle; adjacent means the side that's next to the angle, but that isn't the hypotenuse (the side opposite the 90° angle). Say you have the following right triangle:

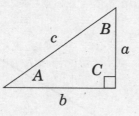

If you want to find the sine of A just think of SOH, and you know you have to divide a, the opposite side, by c, the hypotenuse of the triangle. Get the idea? So in the above:

$$\sin A = \frac{a}{c} \quad \sin B = \frac{b}{c}$$

$$\cos A = \frac{b}{c} \quad \cos B = \frac{a}{c}$$

$$\tan A = \frac{a}{b} \quad \tan B = \frac{b}{a}$$

There are some values for the sine, cosine, and tangent of particular angles that you should memorize for the ACT. ACT trig questions often test these angles, and if you have the trig values memorized, you can save a great deal of time.

Angle	Sine	Cosine	Tangent
0°	0	1	0
30°	$\dfrac{1}{2}$	$\dfrac{\sqrt{3}}{2}$	$\dfrac{\sqrt{3}}{3}$
45°	$\dfrac{\sqrt{2}}{2}$	$\dfrac{\sqrt{2}}{2}$	1
60°	$\dfrac{\sqrt{3}}{2}$	$\dfrac{1}{2}$	$\sqrt{3}$
90°	1	0	undefined

Solving Triangles

Once you understand the trigonometric functions of sine, cosine, and tangent, you should be able to use these functions to "solve" a triangle. In other words, if you are given some information about a triangle, you should be able to use the trigonometric functions to figure out the values of other angles or sides of the triangle. For example:

What is the length of $\overline{BC}$ in the triangle below?

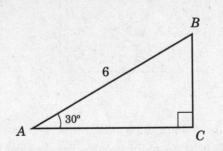

In this problem, you are given the measure of $\angle A$, as well as the length of $\overline{AB}$. The image also shows that this triangle is a right triangle. You can use this information to solve for $\overline{BC}$ if you can figure out which trigonometric function to use. You have to find the value of side $\overline{BC}$, which stands opposite the angle you know. You also know the value of the hypotenuse. To figure out $\overline{BC}$, then, you need to use the trig function that uses both opposite and hypotenuse, which is sine. From the chart of the values of critical points, you know that $\sin \ \sin 30° = \dfrac{1}{2}$.

To solve:

$$\sin 30° = \frac{x}{6}$$

$$\frac{1}{2} = \frac{x}{6}$$

$$x = 3$$

Another favorite ACT problem is to combine the Pythagorean theorem with trig functions, like so:

> What is the sine of $\angle A$ in right triangle ABC below?

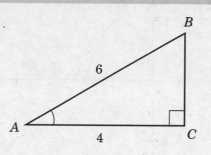

To find the sine of $\angle A$, you need to know the value of the side opposite $\angle A$ and the value of the hypotenuse. The figure gives the value of the hypotenuse, but not of the opposite side. However, since the figure does provide the value of $\overline{AC}$, you can calculate the value of the opposite side, $\overline{BC}$, by using the Pythagorean theorem.

$$AB^2 = AC^2 + BC^2$$
$$6^2 = 4^2 + x^2$$
$$36 = 16 + x^2$$
$$x^2 = 20$$
$$x = \sqrt{20} = 2\sqrt{5}$$

Now that you know the value of $\overline{BC}$, you can solve for sine A:

$$\sin A = \frac{2\sqrt{5}}{6}$$
$$\sin A = \frac{\sqrt{5}}{3}$$

Trigonometric Identities

A trigonometric identity is an equation involving trigonometric functions that holds true for all angles. For the ACT test, trigonometric identities, on those few occasions when they come up, will be helpful in situations when you need to simplify a trigonometric expression. The two identities you should know are:

---

1. $\tan\theta = \dfrac{\sin\theta}{\cos\theta}$

2. $\sin^2\theta + \cos^2\theta = 1$

If you see an expression that contains either $\dfrac{\sin\theta}{\cos\theta}$ or $\sin^2\theta + \cos^2\theta$, you should immediately substitute in its identity.

Trigonometric Graphs

The ACT will include one or two questions covering the graphs of the trigonometric functions. You should be able to match each graph with each function, and you should know when the different functions reach their highest point and lowest point.

Graph of $y = \sin x$

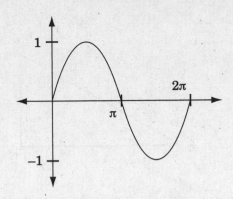

Graph of $y = \cos x$

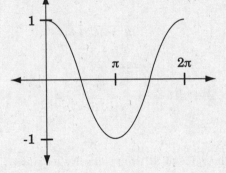

Graph of $y = \tan x$

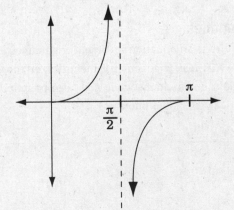

Stretching the Trigonometric Graphs

In addition to knowing the graphs of the trigonometric functions, you should also know how the graphs can be stretched vertically or horizontally. Vertical stretches affect the graph's amplitude, while horizontal stretches change the period.

Stretching the Amplitude

If a coefficient is placed in front of the function, the graph will stretch vertically: Its highest points will be higher and its lowest points will be lower. The function $y = \sin x$ never goes higher than 1 or lower than –1, the function $y = 3 \sin x$ has a high point of 3 and a low point of –3. Changing the amplitude of a function does not change the value of x at which the high and low points occur. In the figure below, for example, $y = \sin x$ and $y = 3 \sin x$ both have their high points when x equals $\frac{-3\pi}{2}$ and $\frac{\pi}{2}$.

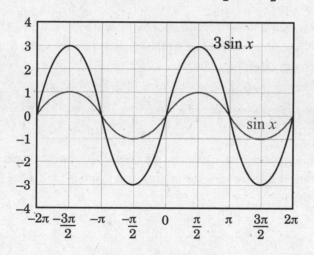

The amplitude of a trigonometric function is equal to the absolute value of the coefficient that appears before the function. The amplitude of $y = 2 \cos x$ is 2, the amplitude of $y = \frac{1}{2} \sin x$ is $\frac{1}{2}$, and the amplitude of $y = -2 \sin x$ is 2.

Stretching the Period

If a coefficient is placed before the x in a trigonometric function, the function is stretched horizontally: Its curves become steeper or less steep depending on the coefficient. The curves of $y = \sin 3x$ are steeper than the curves of $y = \sin \frac{1}{2}x$. This coefficient doesn't affect the amplitude of the function in any way, but it does affect *where* on the x-axis the function has its high and low points. The figure on the next page shows how changing the period affects a sine curve.

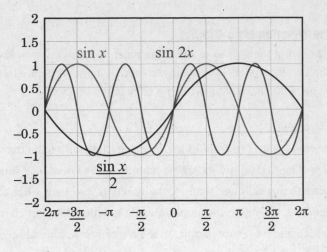

The ACT may test your knowledge of periods by presenting you with a trig function that has a period coefficient and asking you for the smallest positive value where the function reaches its maximum value. For example:

What is the smallest positive value for x where $y = \cos 2x$ reaches its maximum value?

To answer this question, you need to know the original cosine curve and be able to carry out some very easy math. Knowing the original trig graph is the crucial thing; the math, as we said, is easy.

PRACTICE FOR THE ACT MATH TEST

MATHEMATICS TEST

60 Minutes—60 Questions

DIRECTIONS: After solving each problem, pick the correct answer from the five given and fill in the corresponding oval on your answer sheet. Solve as many problems as you can in the time allowed. Do not worry over problems that take too much time; skip them if necessary and return to them if you have time.

Calculator use is permitted on the test. Calculators can be used for any problem on the test, though calculators may be more harm than help for some questions.

Note: unless otherwise stated on the test, you should assume that:

1. Figures accompanying questions are not drawn to scale.
2. Geometric figures exist in a plane.
3. When given in a question, "line" refers to a straight line.
4. When given in a question, "average" refers to the arithmetic mean.

PRACTICE SET 1: PRE-ALGEBRA

---

1. Samantha had 3 more cookies than Arthur. Then Arthur gave her 4 of his cookies. Now how many more cookies does Samantha have than Arthur?
   A. 8
   B. 9
   C. 10
   D. 11
   E. 12

2. The daily totals of dinner customers served at the Little Chef restaurant last Tuesday through Sunday were 232, 263, 298, 472, 451, and 372. What was the average number of lunch customers served each day?
   F. 2,088
   G. 872
   H. 567
   J. 451
   K. 348

3. Adrian has 5 striped shirts and 6 solid-colored shirts hanging together in his closet. In his haste to get to his appointment, he randomly grabs 1 of these 11 shirts. What is the probability the shirt that Adrian grabs is solid-colored?

    A. $\dfrac{1}{5}$

    B. $\dfrac{5}{6}$

    C. $\dfrac{1}{11}$

    D. $\dfrac{5}{11}$

    E. $\dfrac{6}{11}$

4. A package of 12 pencils is priced at \$1.20 now. If the pencils go on sale for 25% off the current price, what will be the sale price of the package?

    F. \$0.60
    G. \$0.70
    H. \$0.80
    J. \$0.90
    K. \$1.00

5. What is the 317th digit after the decimal point in the repeating decimal $0.6\overline{8423}$?
    A. 8
    B. 6
    C. 4
    D. 3
    E. 2

6. What is the value of $|9 - x|$ if $x = 11$?
    F. −2
    G. −1
    H. 1
    J. 2
    K. 3

7. $\dfrac{1}{4} \cdot \dfrac{2}{5} \cdot \dfrac{3}{6} \cdot \dfrac{4}{7} \cdot \dfrac{5}{8} \cdot \dfrac{6}{9} \cdot \dfrac{7}{10} \cdot \dfrac{8}{11} = ?$ $\dfrac{6}{990} = \dfrac{2}{330}$

    A. $\dfrac{2}{15}$

    B. $\dfrac{1}{99}$

    C. $\dfrac{1}{165}$

    D. 2

    E. $\dfrac{11}{2}$

8. On the real number line below, numbers increase in value from left to right, and C is negative. The value of B must be:

left B C right

F. positive
G. negative
H. greater than C
J. between 0 and C
K. equal to 0

9. Marissa has a basket of red, yellow, and pink roses in a ratio of 6:3:2. The basket contains a total of 44 roses. How many pink roses are in the basket?
A. 2
B. 6
C. 8
D. 12
E. 14

10. Charles A. Lindbergh's airplane *Spirit of St. Louis* was 27 feet, 8 inches long, with a 46-foot wingspan. If you are making a $\dfrac{1}{15}$ scale model of this airplane, what should be the length of the model's wingspan, in feet?

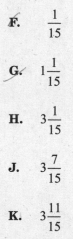

F. $\dfrac{1}{15}$

G. $1\dfrac{1}{15}$

H. $3\dfrac{1}{15}$

J. $3\dfrac{7}{15}$

K. $3\dfrac{11}{15}$

11. Delivery costs for Ocean Beach Hardware increased by 45% because the store moved further away from the warehouse. If it cost Ocean Beach Hardware $90 to ship tools before the store moved, how much would it cost to ship the same tools after the move?
A. $49.50
B. $62.75
C. $130.50
D. $165.25
E. $180.00

12. $(8d^3 - 3de^2 + 2e) - (6e + 5d^3 + 4de^2)$ is equivalent to:

    F. $2d^3 + 8de^2 + 6e$

    G. $13d^3 - 7de^2 - 4e$

    H. $3d^3 - 7de^2 + 4e$

    J. $13d^3 + de^2 - 4e$

    K. $3d^3 - 8de^2 + 2e$

    $13d^3 + de^2 - 4e$

13. What are the next three numbers in the series $100 + 50 + 25 + \dfrac{25}{2} + \dfrac{25}{4} + \dots$?

    A. $\dfrac{25}{6} + \dfrac{25}{8} + \dfrac{25}{10}$

    B. $\dfrac{25}{8} + \dfrac{25}{16} + \dfrac{25}{32}$

    C. $\dfrac{50}{8} + \dfrac{75}{16} + \dfrac{100}{32}$

    D. $\dfrac{25}{5} + \dfrac{25}{6} + \dfrac{25}{7}$

    E. $\dfrac{50}{6} + \dfrac{75}{8} + \dfrac{100}{10}$

14. What number is a multiple of 12, 16, and 18?

    F.   192

    G.   216

    H.   288

    J.   1,736

    K.   3,455

15. $(-5a^4)^3$ is equivalent to:

    A. $125a^{12}$

    B. $125a^7$

    C. $-5a^{12}$

    D. $-125a^7$

    E. $-125a^{12}$

PRACTICE SET 1: ANSWERS & EXPLANATIONS

1.   **D**   Numbers

     Choose a number of cookies for Arthur. You must choose 4 or more, so that he has
     enough cookies to give Samantha 4. Let's say he has 15 cookies. Samantha has
     3 more cookies than Arthur, so Samantha has 15 + 3 = 18 cookies. After Arthur
     gives Samantha 4 of his cookies, she has 18 + 4 = 22, and he has 15 − 4 = 11. The
     difference between 22 and 11 is 11, so **D** is correct.

2. **K** Mean

The average is found by adding up the numbers you are given (232, 263, 298, 472, 451, and 372) and dividing by the number of numbers you are given (6). Add: 232 + 263 + 298 + 472 + 451 + 372 = 2,088. Divide: 2,088 ÷ 6 = 348. This makes **K** the right answer.

3. **E** Probability

Adrian has 6 chances to choose a solid-colored shirt because there are 6 solid-colored shirts in the closet. There are 5 striped + 6 solid-colored = 11 shirts in the closet all together, so the probability that Adrian grabs a solid-colored shirt is $\dfrac{6}{11}$. This makes **E** correct.

4. **J** Percents

The sale price is 100% − 25% = 75% of the current price. Change 75% to a decimal and multiply it by the current price: (0.75)($1.20) = $0.90, which means **J** is the right answer.

5. **A** Series

Five decimal places repeat, as evidenced by the bar above the digits. Divide: 317 ÷ 5 = 63 with a remainder of 2. This means there are 63 complete repetitions of the 5 digits, and 2 digits are left over. Move 2 digits to the right of the decimal point, and the digit is 8, making **A** correct.

6. **J** Absolute Value

Substitute 11 for x inside the absolute value symbols and simplify:

$$\left|9 - 11\right| = \left|-2\right|$$
$$= 2$$

7. **C** Ratios

Cancel common factors:

$$\frac{1}{\cancel{4}} \cdot \frac{2}{\cancel{5}} \cdot \frac{3}{\cancel{6}} \cdot \frac{\cancel{4}}{\cancel{7}} \cdot \frac{\cancel{5}}{\cancel{8}} \cdot \frac{\cancel{6}}{9} \cdot \frac{\cancel{7}}{10} \cdot \frac{\cancel{8}}{11} = ?$$

Multiply the remaining factors in the numerator and denominator and reduce the fraction:

$$\frac{1 \cdot 2 \cdot 3}{9 \cdot 10 \cdot 11} = \frac{6}{990}$$
$$= \frac{1}{165}$$

8. **G** Numbers

You are told that C is negative. This means that B is also negative because B is to the left of C on the number line. The correct answer is **G**.

9. **C** Ratios

The question lets you know that for every 6 red roses, you also have 3 yellow and 2 pink roses. This means that out of every 11 roses, 2 of them will be pink. Set up a proportion:

$$\frac{2}{11} = \frac{x}{44}$$

$$88 = 11x$$

$$x = 8$$

10. **H** Ratios

A scale of $\frac{1}{15}$ means that 1 inch on the scale model represents 15 inches on the real airplane. Multiply 46 feet by $\frac{1}{15}$:

$$46 \times \frac{1}{5} = \frac{46}{15}$$

$$= 3\frac{1}{15}$$

11. **C** Percents

An increase of 45% means the new delivery cost is 100% + 45% = 145% of the current cost. Turn this percent into a decimal number and multiply by $90 to find the new delivery cost: (1.45)($90) = $130.50. This means that **C** is the right answer.

12. **J** Exponents

Write the first trinomial without parentheses. Then distribute the negative sign between the parentheses across each term in the second set of parentheses:

$$(8d^3 - 3de^2 + 2e) - (6e - 5d^3 - 4de^2) = 8d^3 - 3de^2 + 2e - 6e + 5d^3 + 4de^2$$

Combine like terms and simplify:

$$(8d^3 + 5d^3) + (-3de^2 + 4de^2) + (+2e - 6e) = 13d^3 + de^2 - 4e$$

13. **B** Series

Notice that to get from one term in the series to the next you must divide by 2, or multiply by $\frac{1}{2}$. Multiply the last term by $\frac{1}{2}$ to get the next term:

$$\frac{25}{4} \cdot \frac{1}{2} = \frac{25}{8}$$

The only answer that starts with $\frac{25}{8}$ is **B.**

14. **H** Multiples

The numbers you are working with are 12, 16, and 18. Multiply two of the numbers together and see if the third number divides evenly into the product. Continue the process until you find a number that divides evenly and appears on the list of answer choices.

12 × 16 = 192	12 × 18 = 216	16 × 18 = 288
192 ÷ 18 = 10. 67	216 ÷ 16 = 13. 5	288 ÷ 12 = 24

The number 288 divides 12, 16, and 18 evenly, so it is a multiple. Therefore, **H** is correct.

15. **E** Exponents

The term $-5a^4$ is raised to the 3rd power. By the power rule, -5 is multiplied by itself 3 times, and the exponent of the a term is multiplied by the outside exponent: $(-5)(-5)(-5)(a^4)^3 = -125a^{12}$

PRACTICE SET 2: ELEMENTARY ALGEBRA

1. A Celsius temperature C can be approximated by halving the difference of 32 and the Fahrenheit temperature F. Which of the following expresses this approximation method?

    (Note: The symbol $\approx$ means "is approximately equal to.")

    A. $C \approx 2(F - 32)$

    B. $C \approx 2F - 32$

    C. $C \approx \dfrac{1}{2}\left(F - 32\right)$

    D. $C \approx \dfrac{1}{2}F - 32$

    E. $C \approx (F - 32)^{\frac{1}{2}}$

2. If $x = -5$, what is the value of $\dfrac{x^2 - 9}{x + 3}$?

    F. -8

    G. -6

    H. 5

    J. $6\dfrac{2}{3}$

    K. 7

3. For all x and y, $(3x + y)(x^2 - y) = ?$
    A. $3x^2 - y^2$
    B. $3x^3 - y^2$
    C. $3x^3 + xy - y^2$
    D. $3x^3 - 3xy - x^2y^2$
    E. $3x^3 + x^2y - 3xy - y^2$

4. In the formula $A = P(1 + rt)$, A is the principal plus simple interest, P is the principal, r is the interest rate expressed as a decimal number, and t is time in years. Which of the following solves this formula for t?

F. $t = \dfrac{A+P}{Pr}$

$t = \dfrac{A}{PR} - \dfrac{P}{PR}$

G. $t = \dfrac{A-P}{P+r}$

H. $t = \dfrac{A-P}{P-r}$

J. $t = \dfrac{A}{r}$

K. $t = \dfrac{A-P}{Pr}$

5. For all x, $8 - 7(x - 4) = ?$
   A. $-7x + 36$
   B. $-7x + 20$ $8 - 7x + 28$
   C. $-7x - 28$
   D. $6x - 20$ $36 - 7x$
   E. $6x - 28$

6. When $x = \dfrac{1}{3}$, what is the value of $\dfrac{9x-2}{x}$?

   F. -30 3

   G. -3

   H. $-\dfrac{1}{3}$

   J. 1

   K. 3

7. What value of x will satisfy the equation $0.2(2x + 1{,}470) = x$?
   A. $2{,}940$
   B. $2{,}130$ $2x + 1470 = 5x$
   C. $1{,}470$
   D. 560 $1470 = 3x$
   E. 490

8. $\dfrac{4z}{7} + \dfrac{4r}{3}$ is equivalent to:

F. $\dfrac{16rz}{21}$

G. $\dfrac{28r + 12z}{10}$

H. $\dfrac{12z + 4r}{3}$

J. $\dfrac{12z + 28r}{7}$

K. $\dfrac{12z + 28r}{21}$

9. Sagan, Alex, and Lindsay were eating a round birthday cake. If Sagan ate 3 slices, Alex ate 5 slices, Lindsay ate 1 slice, and 1 more than one-third of the slices remain, into how many slices was the original cake cut?

A. 12
B. 13
C. 14
D. 15
E. 16

10. If $\dfrac{5}{6}x - 4 > -11$, what is the set of all possible values of x?

F. $x > \dfrac{6}{5}$

G. $x < -\dfrac{66}{5}$

H. $x < -\dfrac{7}{6}$

J. $x > \dfrac{24}{5}$

K. $x > -\dfrac{42}{5}$

11. The length a of the ship *Amazon Queen* is 30 feet more than four-fifths the length w of the *Arctic Wolf*. Which of the following expresses the relationship between a and w?

    A. $a = \dfrac{4}{5}w - 30$

    B. $w = \dfrac{4}{5}a + 30$

    C. $w = \dfrac{4}{5}w - 30$

    D. $a = \dfrac{4}{5}w + 30$

    E. $a + 30 = \dfrac{4}{5}w + 30$

12. For all a and b, $(2a + 4b)(2a - 4b) = ?$
    F. $4(a^2 + 4ab - 4b^2)$
    G. $2a^2 + 4ab + b^2$
    H. $2(a^2 + b^2)$
    J. $4(a^2 - 4b^2)$
    K. $2(a^2 + 4ab - b^2)$

13. For $-16 \leq x - 8 < 24$, what are the possible values of x?
    A. $-8 \leq x < 16$
    B. $-24 \leq x < 16$
    C. $-8 \leq x < 32$
    D. $-16 < x \leq 24$
    E. $-8 \geq x > 32$

14. Which of the following is the factorization of the binomial $x^2 - 4^2$?
    F. $x(x + 2x + 2)$
    G. $(x - 4)^2$
    H. $(x + 4)(x + 2)$
    J. $(x - 4)(x + 4)$
    K. $(x + 4)^2$

15. A bus drove for 6 hours at a speed of x miles per hour (mph) and for 8 more hours at 60 mph. If the average speed for the entire trip was 58 mph, which of the following equations could be used to find x?
    A. $x + 60 = 58(2)$
    B. $x + 60(8) = 58(14)$
    C. $6x - 60(8) = 58(14)$
    D. $6x + 60(8) = 58(2)$
    E. $6x + 60(8) = 58(14)$

PRACTICE SET 2: ANSWERS & EXPLANATIONS

1. **C** Expressions

    To halve something, you need to either divide by 2 or multiply by $\frac{1}{2}$. **C** and **D** are the only choices that multiply by $\frac{1}{2}$, so you can eliminate **A**, **B**, and **E**.

    You need to multiply the *difference* of F and 32 by $\frac{1}{2}$, so eliminate **D** because only F is multiplied by $\frac{1}{2}$. This leaves **C** as the correct answer.

2. **F** Substitution

    Substitute −5 in place of the x in the numerator and denominator and simplify:

    $$\frac{(-5)^2 - 9}{-5 + 3} = \frac{25 - 9}{-2}$$
    $$= \frac{16}{-2}$$
    $$= -8$$

3. **E** Binomials

    Multiply the two binomials using the FOIL method: first terms, outer terms, inner terms, last terms. Write the products in alphabetical order.

    First: $(3x)(x^2) = 3x^3$
    Outer: $(3x)(-y) = -3xy$
    Inner: $(y)(x^2) = x^2y$
    Last: $(y)(-y) = -y^2$

    Write the terms in descending order on the x term: $3x^3 + x^2y - 3xy - y^2$. **E** is the correct answer.

4. **K** Expressions

    Start solving for t by distributing P across $(1 + rt)$. Continue solving for t as follows:

Original equation	$A = P(1 + rt)$
Distribute P across $(1 + rt)$	$A = P + Prt$
Subtract P from both sides	$A - P = Prt$
Divide by Pr	$\dfrac{A - P}{Pr} = \dfrac{Prt}{Pr}$
Simplify	$\dfrac{A - P}{Pr} = t$

5. **A** Simplification

    By the order of operations, you must distribute 7 across $(x - 4)$, then combine like terms and simplify:

    $$8 - 7(x - 4) = ?$$
    $$8 - 7x + 28 = ?$$
    $$-7x + 36 = ?$$

6. **K** Substitution

Substitute $\dfrac{1}{3}$ in place of the x in both places where it appears and simplify:

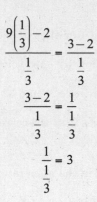

$$\frac{9\left(\dfrac{1}{3}\right)-2}{\dfrac{1}{3}}=\frac{3-2}{\dfrac{1}{3}}$$

$$\frac{3-2}{\dfrac{1}{3}}=\frac{1}{\dfrac{1}{3}}$$

$$\frac{1}{\dfrac{1}{3}}=3$$

The correct answer is **K**.

7. **E** Linear Equations

Solve for x. Start by distributing 0.2 across $(2x + 1{,}470)$. Then solve for x:
(Subtract 0.4)

$$0.2\left(2x+1{,}470\right)=x$$

$$0.4x+294=1x$$

$$\underline{-0.4x\qquad -0.4x}$$

$$\frac{294}{0.6}=\frac{0.6x}{0.6}$$

$$490=x$$

8. **K** Simplification

You must identify a common denominator before you can add the fractions. The least common denominator is $7 \times 3 = 21$. Multiply the first fraction by $\dfrac{3}{3}$ and the second fraction by $\dfrac{7}{7}$ to get a common denominator of 21. Then simplify:

$$\left(\frac{4z}{7}\right)\left(\frac{3}{3}\right)+\left(\frac{4r}{3}\right)\left(\frac{7}{7}\right)=\frac{12z}{21}+\frac{28r}{21}$$

$$=\frac{12z+28r}{21}$$

9. **D** Linear Equations

Let x represent the number of slices in the whole cake. Add the number of slices given in the problem and set the sum equal to x. Then solve for x:

$$3+5+1+\left(\frac{1}{3}x+1\right)=x$$

$$10+\frac{1}{3}x=1x$$

$$-\frac{1}{3}x-\frac{1}{3}x \quad \text{Subtract } \frac{1}{3}$$

$$10=\frac{2}{3}x$$

$$\frac{3}{2}(10)=x$$

$$\frac{30}{2}=x$$

$$15=x$$

10. **K** Inequalities

Solve for x:

$$\frac{5}{6}x-4>-11$$

$$+4 \qquad +4 \qquad \text{Add 4 to both sides.}$$

$$\frac{5}{6}x>-7$$

$$\left(\frac{6}{5}\right)\frac{5}{6}x>-7\left(\frac{6}{5}\right)$$

$$x>-\frac{42}{5}$$

11. **D** Expressions

Translate the sentence into a math equation: "The length of the ship *Amazon Queen*" is represented by "a," and the word "is" means "=." The expression "30 feet more than" means you add 30 feet to whatever comes next. "Four-fifths" is written as the fraction "$\frac{4}{5}$" "of" means multiplication, and "the length of the *Arctic Wolf*" is represented by "w." Put the terms together in a math equation:

$$a=\frac{4}{5}w+30$$

12. **J** Binomials

Multiply the binomials using the FOIL method:

$$(2a+4b)(2a-4b)=4a^2-8ab+8ab-16b^2$$

The middle terms cancel out, leaving $4a^2-16b^2$. Factor out the 4:

$$4a^2-16b^2=4(a^2-4b^2)$$

13. **C** Inequalities

Add 8 to the center and each side of the inequality symbols to get the x term alone:

$$-16 \leq x - 8 < 24$$
$$ +8 +8 \phantom{<} +8$$
$$-8 \leq x < 32$$

14. **J** Binomials

This binomial is the difference of two squares. The formula for the difference of two squares is $a^2 - b^2 = (a - b)(a + b)$. In this problem, $a = x$ and $b = 4$. Substitute x for a and 4 for b in the formula and simplify:

$$a^2 - b^2 = (a - b)(a + b)$$
$$x^2 - 4^2 = (x - 4)(x + 4)$$

15. **E** Expressions

This is a rate × time = distance problem. The rate × time for the first part of the trip is x times 6, or $6x$. The rate × time for the second part of the trip is 60 mph times 8 hours, or $(60)(8)$. The total distance is the average speed times the sum of the hours, or $58(6 + 8)$. The equation is:

$$6x + 60(8) = 58(14)$$

PRACTICE SET 3: INTERMEDIATE ALEGBRA

1. Which of the following is a factor of the quadratic equation $x^2 - 2x - 24 = 0$?

   A. $x + 4$

   B. $x + 6$

   C. $x + 2$

   D. $x - 4$

   E. $x - 2$

2. The flight of a projectile is modeled by the function $h = -16t^2 + 48t + 64$, where h is the height above the ground measured in feet, and t represents time in flight measured in seconds. According to this model, the projectile will hit the ground when $t =$?

   F. 2

   G. 3

   H. 4

   J. 4.6

   K. 5.2

3. The *range* of a function f is the set of all values of y for which $f(x)$ is defined. One of the following sets is the range for the function graphed below. Which set is that range?

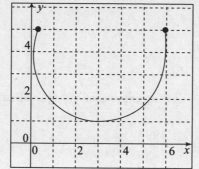

  A. $\{1, 2, 3, 4, 5\}$
  B. $\{0.2, 1, 2, 3, 4, 5, 5, 8\}$
  C. $\{x \mid 0.2 \leq x \leq 5.0\}$
  D. $\{x \mid 1 \leq y \leq 5\}$
  E. $\{y \mid 0 \leq y \leq 5\}$

4. If $f(x) = 2(x^2 + 7)$, then $f(a + b) = ?$
  F. $2a^2 + 2b^2 + 14$
  G. $2a^2 + 4ab + 2b^2 + 14$
  H. $a^2 + 2ab + b^2 + 14$
  J. $2a^2 + 2ab + 2b^2 + 14$
  K. $a^2 + 4ab + 14$

5. The distance a spring stretches, d, varies directly as the weight, w, attached to it. If a weight of 130 pounds stretches a spring 13 inches from its equilibrium point, what distance will the spring stretch if a weight of 40 pounds is placed on it?
  A. 1
  B. 2
  C. 3
  D. 4
  E. 5

6. If $c + 4d = 8$ and $8c - 9d = -18$, what is the value of $c + d$?
  F. 0
  G. 2
  H. 4
  J. 5
  K. 7

7. If $f(x) = x^2 + 3$ and $g(x) = x - 4$, which of the following shows the value of $(f \circ g)(x)$?
  A. $x^2 - 8x + 13$
  B. $x^2 - 8x - 13$
  C. $x^2 - 1$
  D. $x^2 + 1$
  E. $x^2 - 8x + 19$

8. If $\log_a 27 = 3$, what is the value of a?

    F.   3

    G.   5

    H.   9

    J.   12

    K.   24

9. If $b = 4$, which of the following expressions is equivalent to b?

    A. $\log_{10} 10{,}000$

    B. $\log_{10} 2$

    C. $\log_2 8$

    D. $\log_{25} 100$

    E. $\log_4 400$

10. Let matrix $A = \begin{bmatrix} 3 & 5 \\ -4 & 7 \end{bmatrix}$ and matrix $B = \begin{bmatrix} 2 & -1 \\ 6 & 8 \end{bmatrix}$. Which of the following matrices shows $A + B$?

    F. $\begin{bmatrix} 1 & 6 \\ -10 & -1 \end{bmatrix}$

    G. $\begin{bmatrix} 5 & 4 \\ 2 & 15 \end{bmatrix}$

    H. $\begin{bmatrix} -5 & 9 \\ 48 & -29 \end{bmatrix}$

    J. $\begin{bmatrix} -21 & 35 \\ -13 & 8 \end{bmatrix}$

    K. $\begin{bmatrix} 5 & 6 \\ -2 & 1 \end{bmatrix}$

11. Let matrix $A = \begin{bmatrix} -2 & 3 \\ 5 & -8 \end{bmatrix}$ and matrix $B = \begin{bmatrix} -1 & 3 \\ -3 & 4 \end{bmatrix}$. Which of the following matrices shows $B - A$?

   A. $\begin{bmatrix} -2 & -3 \\ 27 & 8 \end{bmatrix}$

   B. $\begin{bmatrix} -1 & 0 \\ 8 & -12 \end{bmatrix}$

   C. $\begin{bmatrix} -3 & 6 \\ 2 & -12 \end{bmatrix}$

   D. $\begin{bmatrix} 10 & 21 \\ 27 & 56 \end{bmatrix}$

   E. $\begin{bmatrix} 1 & 0 \\ -8 & 12 \end{bmatrix}$

12. Given the function $f(x) = 3x^2 - 18x + 33$, what is the value of $f(x)$ when $x = 2$?

   F. 3
   G. 6
   H. 9
   J. 10
   K. 12

13. What is the solution to this system of linear equations?

$$4x + 3y = 9$$
$$x - 2y = 5$$

   A. $(2, -5)$
   B. $(-1, 3)$
   C. $(3, -1)$
   D. all real numbers
   E. no solution

14. Newbreak Coffee Company baristas mix Arabian Mocha Java and Colombian coffees together to make the store's Sunrise Blend. Three pounds of Arabian Mocha Java plus five pounds of Colombian cost $73. Four pounds of Arabian Mocha Java plus eight pounds of Colombian cost $110. Let a = price per pound of Arabian Mocha Java and c = price per pound of Colombian. What is the price per pound (a, c) of the two types of coffee?

   F. ($9.75, $10.50)
   G. ($8.50, $9.50)
   H. ($12.50, $10.50)
   J. ($10.50, $9.75)
   K. ($9.50, $8.50)

15. Which of the following are the solutions of $6x^2 - 11x - 10 = 0$?

A. $-\dfrac{2}{3}, \dfrac{5}{2}$

B. $\dfrac{5}{3}, -1$

C. $-\dfrac{1}{3}, 5$

D. $-\dfrac{5}{3}, 1$

E. $-\dfrac{5}{2}, \dfrac{2}{3}$

PRACTICE SET 3: ANSWERS & EXPLANATIONS

1. **A** Quadratics
   Factor $x^2 - 2x - 24$ by first finding the factors of the last term, -24, that add up
   to the coefficient on the x term, -2. The factors are -6 and 4 because $-6 + 4 = -2$.
   Next, write the quadratic equation in factored form: $x^2 - 2x - 24 = (x - 6)(x + 4)$.
   The answer choice that matches one of these factors is **A**.

2. **H** Quadratics
   When the projectile hits the ground, its height is 0 feet. Substitute 0 for h in the
   equation and solve for t:

Original equation	$h = -16t^2 + 48t + 64$
Set $h = 0$	$0 = -16t^2 + 48t + 64$
Factor out -16	$0 = -16(t^2 - 3t - 4)$
Factor $t^2 - 3t - 4$	$0 = -16(t - 4)(t + 1)$

   For the last equation to be true, t must equal 4 or -1. Since time cannot be negative, 4 seconds is the correct answer, which is **H**.

3. **D** Functions
   The graph is a curve, so the range includes *all* values of y from the smallest to the
   largest, including the smallest and largest. The smallest value of y is 1, and the
   largest value is 5. All values between 1 and 5 are also included, so the range is
   $\{y \mid 1 \le y \le 5\}$, making **D** correct.

4. **G** Functions
   Substitute $(a + b)$ for x in the function and solve:

$$f(x) = 2(x^2 + 7)$$
$$f(a+b) = 2[(a+b)^2 + 7]$$
$$= 2[(a+b)(a+b)+7]$$
$$= 2[a^2+ab+ab+b^2+7]$$
$$= 2[a^2+2ab+b^2+7]$$
$$= 2a^2+4ab+2b^2+14$$

5. **D** Relationships

Set up the equation of direct variation: $d = kw$. Substitute 13 for d and 130 for w and solve for k:

$$d = kw$$
$$13 = k(130)$$
$$10 = k$$

Now that you know k, set up the equation again and solve for d:

$$d = kw$$
$$d = (0.1)(40)$$
$$d = 4$$

6. **G** Systems of Equations

Solve the first equation for c:

$$c+4d=8$$
$$c=8-4d$$

Substitute $8 - 4d$ for c in the second equation:

$$8c-9d=-18$$
$$8(8-4d)-9d=-18$$
$$64-32d-9d=-18$$
$$-41d=-82$$
$$d=2$$

Substitute 2 for d in the first equation, and solve for c:

$$c+4d=8$$
$$c+4(2)=8$$
$$c=0$$

The sum of $c + d$ is 0 + 2, or 2.

7. **E** Functions

This is a compound function and can be written as $f(g(x))$. Replace $g(x)$ with $x - 4$ and find the function value $f(x - 4)$:

$$f(x-4)=(x-4)^2+3$$
$$= x^2-8x+16+3$$
$$= x^2-8x+19$$

8. **F** Logarithms

The logarithmic equation $\log_a x = b$ is equivalent to the exponential equation $x = a^b$. In this equation $\log_a 27 = 3$, $x = 27$ and $b = 3$. Substitute 27 for x and 3 for b into the exponential equation:

$$x = a^b$$
$$27 = a^3$$

Next, solve for a:

$$\sqrt[3]{27} = \sqrt[3]{a}$$
$$3 = a$$

9. **A** Logarithms

The logarithmic equation $\log_a x = b$ is equivalent to the exponential equation $x = a^b$. Substitute 4 for b in the exponential equation:

$$x = a^4$$

You're looking for a number, a, that yields a number, x, when raised to the fourth power. Check each answer choice, starting with **A**. In the expression $\log_{10} 10,000$, 10 $= a$ and $10,000 = x$. Substitute 10 for a and 10,000 for x in the exponential equation:

$$x = a^4$$
$$10,000 = 10^4$$

So **A** is correct.

10. **G** Matrices

Add together the corresponding entries. The entries in the first row are $3 + 2 = 5$ and $5 + (-1) = 4$. The entries in the second row are $(-4) + 6 = 2$ and $7 + 8 = 15$. So, the resulting matrix is:

$$A + B = \begin{bmatrix} 5 & 4 \\ 2 & 15 \end{bmatrix}$$

11. **E** Matrices

Subtract the corresponding entries. The entries in the first row are $-1 - (-2) = 1$ and $3 - 3 = 0$. The entries in the second row are $(-3) - 5 = -8$ and $4 - (-8) = 12$. So, the resulting matrix is:

$$B - A = \begin{bmatrix} 1 & 0 \\ -8 & 12 \end{bmatrix}$$

12. **H** Functions

Substitute 2 for x into the function and solve:

$$f(x) = 3x^2 - 18x + 33$$
$$= 3(2)^2 - 18(2) + 33$$
$$= 3(4) - 36 + 33$$
$$= 12 - 36 + 33$$
$$= 9$$

13. **C** Systems of Equations

Solve by the substitution method. Solve the second equation for x:

$$x - 2y = 5$$
$$x = 5 + 2y$$

Substitute $5 + 2y$ into the first equation in place of x and solve for y:

$$4x + 3y = 9$$
$$4(5 + 2y) + 3y = 9$$
$$20 + 8y + 3y = 9$$
$$20 + 11y = 9$$
$$11y = -11$$
$$y = -1$$

Substitute -1 in place of y in the equation for x and solve for x:

$$x = 5 + 2(-1)$$
$$x = 3$$

The solution to the system of equations is $(3, -1)$, which is **C**.

14. **G** Systems of Equations

Write a system of equations to represent the problem, where a = price per pound of Arabian Mocha Java and c = price per pound of Colombian:

$$3a + 5c = \$73$$
$$4a + 8c + \$110$$

Solve the system by the elimination method. Multiply each term in the first equation by -4 and each term in the second equation by 3 and then add the equations together to eliminate the variable a:

$$(-4)3a + (-4)5c = (-4)\$73$$
$$(3)4a + (3)8c = (3)\$110$$

$$-12a - 20c = -\$292$$
$$12a + 24c = \$330$$

$$4c = \$38$$
$$c = \$9.50$$

Substitute $\$9.50$ in place of c in the first equation to solve for a:

$$3a + 5(\$9.50) = \$73$$
$$3a + \$47.50 = \$73$$
$$3a = \$25.50$$
$$a = \$8.50$$

The solution is $(\$8.50, \$9.50)$, which is **G**.

15. **A** Quadratics

Look to see if you can divide out a common factor from each term. You can't, so set up two sets of parentheses with the factors of $6x^2$ as the first term in the parentheses and factors of -10 as the second term in the parentheses:

$$(3x - 5)(2x + 2)$$

Distribute using the FOIL method, and simplify to see if you get back to $6x^2 - 11x - 10$:

$$(3x - 5)(2x + 2) = 6x^2 - 4x - 10$$

You do not, so switch the -5 and $+2$ and try again:

$$(3x + 2)(2x - 5) = 6x^2 - 11x - 10$$

This time you get back to the original trinomial. Now set each factor equal to 0 and solve for x.

$$3x + 2 = 0 \qquad\qquad 2x - 5 = 0$$
$$3x = -2 \qquad\qquad 2x = 5$$
$$x = -\frac{2}{3} \qquad\qquad x = \frac{5}{2}$$

These solutions match **A**.

PRACTICE SET 4: COORDINATE GEOMETRY

1. In the standard (x,y) coordinate plane, what is the distance between the points $(7,-3)$ and $(-8,6)$?

    A. 9
    B. $\sqrt{82}$
    C. $3\sqrt{34}$
    D. 36
    E. 64

2. Three distinct lines, all contained in a plane, intersect each of the other two lines in exactly one point per line. How many distinct regions are formed by the three lines?

    F. 3
    G. 4
    H. 5
    J. 6
    K. 7

3. Which of the following graphs is the solution to $-2y - 3 < 7$?

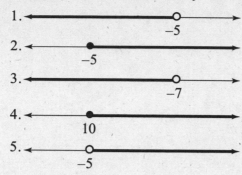

A. 1
B. 2
C. 3
D. 4
E. 5

4. Which of the following graphs is the solution to $|2x - 7| > 5$?

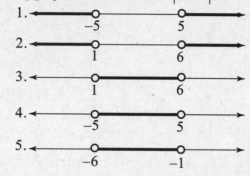

F. 1
G. 2
H. 3
J. 4
K. 5

5. Which of the following graphs is the solution to $-6 < 2x - 12 < 18$?

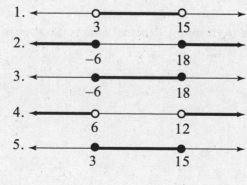

A. 1
B. 2
C. 3
D. 4
E. 5

6. Which of the following equations shows $x + 3y = 5$ written in slope-intercept form?

    F. $y - 0 = -\dfrac{1}{3}(x - 5)$

    G. $y = -\dfrac{1}{3}x + \dfrac{5}{3}$

    H. $y = 3x + 5$

    J. $y = \dfrac{1}{3}x - \dfrac{5}{3}$

    K. $y - \dfrac{7}{3} = -\dfrac{1}{3}(x - 2)$

7. What is the slope of a line that is parallel to $x - 3y = 9$?

    A. $-\dfrac{1}{9}$

    B. $\dfrac{1}{3}$

    C.   3

    D.   6

    E.   9

8. In the standard (x,y) coordinate plane, what is the slope of the line joining the points $(3,-5)$ and $(6,10)$?

    F. -4

    G. -2

    H.   1

    J.   3

    K.   5

9. In the standard (x,y) coordinate plane, what is the slope of the line given by the equation $2x - 7y = 12$?

    A. $-\dfrac{2}{7}$

    B. -2

    C. $\dfrac{2}{7}$

    D. $\dfrac{7}{2}$

    E.   7

10. In the standard (x,y) coordinate plane, what is the slope of the line given by the equation $3x + 5y = 8$?

    F. -5

    G. $-\dfrac{5}{3}$

    H. $-\dfrac{3}{5}$

    J. $\dfrac{3}{5}$

    K. 8

11. In the standard (x,y) coordinate plane, what is the equation of the line that passes through the points $(0,7)$ and $(8,7)$?

    A. $y = -7$
    B. $x = 7$
    C. $y = 7$
    D. $x = -7$
    E. $y = 8$

12. In the standard (x,y) coordinate plane, the slope, m, of a line that goes through the point $(0,0)$ is -1. What is the relationship between the x- and y-coordinates of each point on the line?

    F.   The x-coordinate is twice the y-coordinate.
    G.   The x-coordinate is one-half the y-coordinate.
    H.   The x- and y-coordinates are the same number.
    J.   The y-coordinate is the negative of the x-coordinate.
    K.   The y-coordinate is one-half the x-coordinate.

13. In the standard (x,y) coordinate plane, the y-coordinate of every point on a line is the same as its corresponding x-coordinate. What is the slope of the line?

    A. -2
    B. -1
    C. 1
    D. 2
    E. 3

14. Which of the following best describes the graph of the equation $y = -x^2$?
    F.   It represents a parabola that opens upward.
    G.   It represents a curved line.
    H.   It represents a parabola that opens downward.
    J.   It crosses the y-axis at $y = -1$.
    K.   It crosses the x-axis at $x = 2$.

15. What is the center of the circle with equation $(x + 3)^2 + (y - 4)^2 = 3$ in the standard (x,y) coordinate plane?

A. $(-3,4)$

B. $\left(-\sqrt{3}, \sqrt{3}\right)$

C. $(3,-4)$

D. $\left(\sqrt{3}, -\sqrt{3}\right)$

E. $(3,4)$

PRACTICE SET 4: ANSWERS & EXPLANATIONS

1. **C** Distance and Midpoints

   The formula for the distance between points in a coordinate plane is as follows:

   $$d = \sqrt{(x_2 - x_1)^2 + (y_2 - y_1)^2}$$

   Let $(x_1, y_1) = (7, -3)$, and $(x_2, y_2) = (-8, 6)$. Substitute these coordinates into the formula and simplify:

   $$d = \sqrt{(-8 - 7)^2 + (6 - (-3))^2}$$
   $$d = \sqrt{(-15)^2 + (9)^2}$$
   $$d = \sqrt{225 + 81}$$
   $$d = \sqrt{306}$$
   $$d = \sqrt{9 \cdot 34}$$
   $$d = 3\sqrt{34}$$

2. **K** Coordinate Plane

   You are given the information that three lines intersect the other two lines in one point per line. This means the three lines form a triangle. This breaks the plane into seven distinct regions that are numbered in the diagram below, so the answer is **K**.

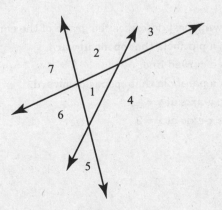

3. **E** Number Lines and Inequalities

You must solve for y and then compare the solution to graphs 1–5:

$$-2y - 3 < 7$$

Add 3 to both sides of the inequality	$+3$ $+3$
Simplify	$-2y < 10$
Divide both sides by	$y > -5$

Notice that the inequality sign reversed direction. When you multiply or divide by a negative number, the inequality sign reverses. The solution is any value greater than (but not equal to) -5. **E** is the correct answer because graph 5 has an open circle on 5 (representing not equal to) and an arrow pointing right (representing greater than [>] -5).

4. **G** Number Lines and Inequalities

The absolute value bars and ">" sign means that $2x - 7$ must be at a distance greater than 5 units from zero. There are two places on the number line where this occurs: to the right of (>) 5 and to the left of (<) -5. Set $2x - 7$ less than -5 and $2x - 7$ greater than 5 and solve for x:

$2x - 7 < -5$		$2x - 7 > 5$
$+7$ $+7$	Add 7 to both sides	$+7$ $+7$
$2x < 2$	Simplify	$2x > 12$
$x < 1$	Divide both sides by 2	$x > 6$

The solutions are all numbers less than 1 and greater than 6. Below is a graph of the result:

This matches graph 2 in the figure, so the correct answer is **G**.

5. **A** Number Lines and Inequalities

Solve the inequality for x:

$$-6 < 2x - 12 < 18$$

Add 12 to the left, center, and right	$+12 +$ $12 + 12$
Simplify	$6 < 2x < 30$
Divide the left, center, and right by 2	$3 < x < 15$

Once x is alone in the center, you can see that x is between 3 and 15. The solution does not include the endpoints 3 and 15 because of the "<" sign. Below is a graph of the result:

This matches graph 1 in the figure, so the correct answer is **A**.

6. **G** Equation of a Line

To write an equation in slope-intercept form, you must solve the equation for y:

$$x + 3y = 5$$

Subtract x from both sides $-x \qquad -x$

Simplify $3y = -x + 5$

Divide both sides by 3 $y = -\dfrac{1}{3}x + \dfrac{5}{3}$

7. **B** Parallel and Perpendicular Lines

Parallel lines have the same slope. Therefore, the slope of a line parallel to $x - 3y = 9$ is the same as the slope of this equation. Solve this equation for y to get it into slope-intercept form ($y = mx + b$). Once you solve for y, the coefficient on the x term is the slope of the line, m:

Multiply both sides by –1 $-1(-3y) = -1(-x + 9)$

Simplify $3y = x - 9$

$$x - 3y = 9$$

Subtract x from each side $-x \qquad -x$

Simplify $-3y = -x + 9$

Divide each term by 3 $y = \dfrac{1}{3}x - 3$

The coefficient on the x term is $\dfrac{1}{3}$, which is the slope of the line, **B**. The slope of a line parallel to this line is also $\dfrac{1}{3}$ because parallel lines have the same slope.

8. **K** Slope

Use the slope formula:

$$m = \frac{y_2 - y_1}{x_2 - x_1}$$

Let $(x_1, y_1) = (3, -5)$ and $(x_2, y_2) = (6, 10)$. Substitute these coordinates into the slope formula and simplify:

$$m = \frac{10 - (-5)}{6 - 3}$$

$$m = \frac{15}{3}$$

$$m = 5$$

9. **C** Equation of a Line

Write the equation in slope-intercept form by solving for y. Once you solve for y, the coefficient on the x term is the slope of the line.

$$2x - 7y = 12$$

Subtract $2x$ from each side $-2x \qquad -2x$

Simplify $-7y = -2x + 12$

Divide each term by -7 $y = \dfrac{2}{7}x - \dfrac{12}{7}$

The coefficient on the x term is $\dfrac{2}{7}$, so the slope of the line is positive and you can eliminate the two negative choices, **A** and **B**. Since the coefficient on the x term represents the slope, m, the slope of the line is $\dfrac{2}{7}$, **C**.

10. **H** Equation of a Line

Write the equation in slope-intercept form by solving for y. Once you solve for y, the coefficient on the x term is the slope of the line.

$$2x - 7y = 12$$

Subtract $2x$ from each side	$-2x \qquad -2x$
Simplify	$-7y = -2x + 12$
Divide each term by -7	$y = \dfrac{2}{7}x - \dfrac{12}{7}$

The coefficient on the x term is $-\dfrac{3}{5}$, so the slope of the line is negative and you can eliminate the two positive choices, **J** and **K**. Since the coefficient on the x term represents the slope, m, the slope of the line is $-\dfrac{3}{5}$, **H**.

11. **C** Equation of a Line

You will first need to use the slope formula to find the slope, m, of the line:

$$m = \frac{y_2 - y_1}{x_2 - x_1}$$

Let $(x_1, y_1) = (0,7)$, and $(x_2, y_2) = (8,7)$. Substitute these coordinates into the slope formula and simplify to find the slope of the line through the two points:

$$m = \frac{7 - 7}{8 - 0}$$

$$m = \frac{0}{8}$$

$$m = 0$$

Next, substitute $(0,7)$ for (x_1, y_1) and 0 for m into the formula for the point-slope form of a line and solve for y:

$$y - y_1 = m(x - x_1)$$

Substitute	$y - 7 = 0(x - 0)$
Simplify	$y - 7 = 0$
Add 7 to both sides	$+7 \quad +7$
Simplify	$y = 7$

The equation of the line through the points $(0,7)$ and $(8,7)$ is $y = 7$, which means the correct answer is **C**.

12. **J** Slope

A slope of −1 means that from the point (0,0) on the line, you can get to another point by moving down 1 (because of the negative sign) and over 1 to the right in the coordinate plane. The coordinates of this new point are (1,−1). If you go down 1 and over 1 to the right again, you are at the point (2,−2). Notice the relationship between the coordinates in each pair: The y-coordinate is the negative of the x-coordinate, which is **J**.

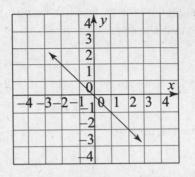

13. **C** Slope

When the y-coordinate of every point on a line is the same as the corresponding x-coordinate, the graph is a diagonal line through the origin.

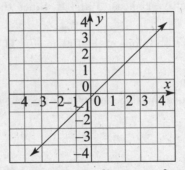

To get from one point with integer coordinates to the next, you must go up 1 and over 1 to the right, which gives the line a positive slope of 1 and makes **C** correct.

14. **H** Graphing Equations

The equation $y = -x^2$ is graphed as a parabola. The negative sign before the x indicates that the parabola opens downward. The parabola crosses the x- and y-axes at the origin. The correct answer is **H**.

15. **A** Conic Sections

The standard equation of a circle is $(x - h)^2 + (y - k)^2 = r^2$, where (h,k) are the coordinates of the center of the circle, and r is the radius of the circle. Write the equation you are given in standard form:

Standard equation of a circle	$(x - h)^2 + (y - k)^2 = r^2$
Equation you are given	$(x + 3)^2 + (y - 4)^2 = 3$
Standard form of the equation you are given	$(x - (-3))^2 + (y - 4)^2 = (\sqrt{3})^2$

You can now see that $h = -3$ and $k = 4$. This means that $(-3,4)$ are the coordinates of the center of the circle, and **A** is the correct answer.

PRACTICE SET 5: PLANE GEOMETRY

1. Marco walks from his house to a friend's house by traveling 10 blocks north and then 8 blocks east. If he cut across a field, he could go in a straight line from his house to his friend's house and save time. Which of the following gives the distance of the straight line from Marco's house to his friend's house?
   A.   9.9
   B.   10.1
   C.   11.6
   D.   12.8
   E.   13.3

2. The diameter of a circle is 12 inches. What is its area, in inches?
   F.   18.9
   G.   37.7
   H.   113.1
   J.   335.6
   K.   452.4

3. In △ABC shown below, the measure of $\overline{AC}$ is 10 inches and $\overline{AB}$ is $5\sqrt{13}$ inches. What is the measure of $\overline{BC}$ in inches?

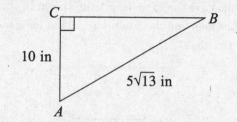

   A.   12
   B.   15
   C. $\sqrt{325}$
   D.   10
   E. $5\sqrt{15}$

4. Which of the following is the volume of the rectangular solid shown below?

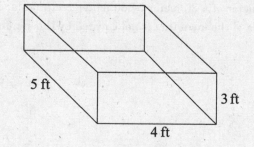

   F.   12
   G.   20
   H.   23
   J.   50
   K.   60

5. The area of a rectangle is 48 in². Which of the following is a possibility for the perimeter of the rectangle?
    A. 26
    B. 34
    C. 40
    D. 52
    E. 96

6. The area of a parallelogram may be found by using the formula $A = bh$, where b is the length of one pair of parallel sides and h is the perpendicular distance between them. What is the area of the parallelogram shown in the figure below?

    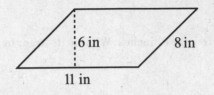

    F. 19
    G. 34
    H. 48
    J. 66
    K. 88

7. All sides of a rhombus are the same length, as shown in the figure below. If one diagonal is 12 inches long and the other is 16 inches long, how many inches long is each side of the rhombus?

    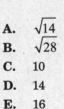

    A. $\sqrt{14}$
    B. $\sqrt{28}$
    C. 10
    D. 14
    E. 16

8. A circular tile sundial with a diameter of 15 meters is placed flat on the ground within the perimeter of a 30 meter by 60 meter rectangular lawn. What is the approximate area of the lawn that is not covered by the sundial?
    F. 75
    G. 1,093
    H. 1,575
    J. 1,623
    K. 1,800

9. What are the measures of the two angles shown in the figure below?

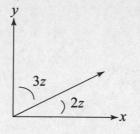

    A.   36°, 54°
    B.   18°, 72°
    C.   36°, 144°
    D.   27°, 63°
    E.   72°, 108°

10. In the figure below, a square with sides of length 6 inches is inscribed in a circle. What is the diameter of the circle?

    F.   6
    G.   12
    H.   36
    J. $2\sqrt{3}$
    K. $6\sqrt{2}$

11. A red circle of fabric is to be sewn onto a rectangular white flag that is 9 feet by 12 feet. The edge of the circle must be at least 3 feet from any edge of the white fabric. What is the maximum radius of a red circle that can be sewn on the flag?

    A.   1.5
    B.   2
    C.   2.5
    D.   3
    E.   3.5

12. In △ABC shown below, $\overline{AB} \cong \overline{AC}$, and the measure of ∠B is 35°. What is the measure of ∠A?

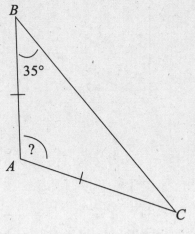

F. 35°
G. 70°
H. 110°
J. 115°
K. 120°

13. In the figure below, $\overline{JM}$, $\overline{KN}$, and $\overline{LQ}$ all intersect at point P, with angle measures as marked. What is the measure of ∠LPN?

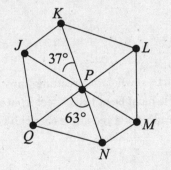

A. 26°
B. 80°
C. 100°
D. 108°
E. 117°

14. The area of the living room in a house is to be tripled. Before construction, the room is 12 feet by 16 feet. If the width is increased by 4 feet, by how many feet must the length increase?

F. 18
G. 20
H. 24
J. 28
K. 36

15. In the figure showing $\triangle CDE$ below, line m is parallel to line n. Which of the following angles must be supplementary to $\angle x$?

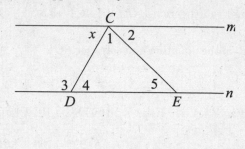

   A. $\angle 1$
   B. $\angle 2$
   C. $\angle 3$
   D. $\angle 4$
   E. $\angle 5$

PRACTICE SET 5: ANSWERS & EXPLANATIONS

1.   **D**   Triangles

This problem describes a right triangle, so you can solve it by setting up the Pythagorean theorem. The straight-line distance squared is equal to 10 squared plus 8 squared:

$$d^2 = 10^2 + 8^2$$
$$d^2 = 100 + 64$$
$$d^2 = 164$$
$$d = 12.8$$

2.   **H**   Circles

The area of a circle is given by the formula $A = \pi r^2$, where $\pi = \dfrac{22}{7}$ (or approximately 3.14159), and r is the radius of the circle. The radius of a circle is half the diameter:

$$r = \frac{1}{2}(12 \text{ inches})$$
$$r = 6 \text{ inches}$$

Substitute $\pi = \dfrac{22}{7}$ and $r = 6$ inches into the formula for area and simplify:

$$A = \pi r^2$$
$$A = \frac{22}{7}\left(6 \text{ inches}\right)^2$$
$$A = \frac{22}{7}\left(36 \text{ square inches}\right)$$
$$A \approx 113.1 \text{ square inches}$$

3.   **B**   Triangles

Set up the Pythagorean theorem: $\left(\overline{AB}\right)^2 = \left(\overline{AC}\right)^2 + \left(\overline{BC}\right)^2$. Substitute 10 for $\overline{AC}$

and $5\sqrt{13}$ for $\overline{AB}$ in the equation and solve for $\overline{BC}$:

$$\left(\overline{AB}\right)^2 = \left(\overline{AC}\right)^2 + \left(\overline{BC}\right)^2$$

Substitute $\qquad\qquad \left(5\sqrt{13}\right)^2 = 10^2 + \left(\overline{BC}\right)^2$

Simplify $\qquad\qquad\qquad 325 = 100 + \left(\overline{BC}\right)^2$

Subtract 100 from both sides $\qquad 225 = \left(\overline{BC}\right)^2$

Take the square root of both sides $\qquad 15 = \overline{BC}$

4.   **K**   Three Dimensions

The volume of a rectangular solid is found by multiplying the length, width, and height:

$$V = lwh$$

Substitute 5 ft for length, 4 ft for width, and 3 ft for height into the formula and simplify:

$$V = lwh$$
$$V = (5 \text{ ft})(4 \text{ ft})(3 \text{ ft})$$
$$V = 60 \text{ ft}^3$$

5.   **D**   Polygons

The formula for the area of a rectangle is $A = lw$, and the formula for the perimeter of a rectangle is $P = 2l + 2w$, where l = length and w = width. Write the possible integer products of 48 as lengths and widths, where the length is greater than or equal to the width. Then write the perimeters that correspond to those lengths and widths. When you find a perimeter that matches one of the answer choices, choose it and move on to the next question.

$A = 48 \times 1$	$A = 24 \times 2$	$A = 16 \times 3$	$A = 12 \times 4$	$A = 8 \times 6$
$P = 2(48) + 2(1)$	$P = 2(24) + 2(2)$	$P = 2(16) + 2(3)$	$P = 2(12) + 2(4)$	$P = 2(8) + 2(6)$
$= 96 + 2$	$= 48 + 4$	$= 32 + 6$	$= 24 + 8$	$= 16 + 12$
$= 98$	$= 52$	$= 38$	$= 32$	$= 28$

The perimeter 52 matches **D**.

6. **J** Polygons

The formula for the area of a parallelogram is $A = bh$. The base and height are always perpendicular to each other. In this parallelogram, the base $b = 11$ in. and the height $h = 6$ in. Substitute these values into the formula for the area of a parallelogram and simplify:

$$A = bh$$
$$A = (11 \text{ in.})(6 \text{in.})$$
$$A = 66 \text{ in}^2$$

7. **C** Polygons

Draw a picture of the rhombus and draw in the diagonals:

The diagonals form 4 right triangles. The long side of each right triangle has a length of $16 \div 2 = 8$, and the short side has a length of $12 \div 2 = 6$. Use the Pythagorean theorem ($c^2 = a^2 + b^2$) to find the length of the hypotenuse of the right triangle, which is equal to the length of the side of the rhombus:

Pythagorean theorem	$c^2 = a^2 + b^2$
Substitute, where $s = $ length of the side of the rhombus	$s^2 = 8^2 + 6^2$
Simplify	$s^2 = 64 + 36$
Simplify	$s^2 = 100$
Take the square root of both sides	$s = 10$

8. **J** Circles

Find the area of the rectangular lawn ($A = lw$) and subtract the area of the circular sundial ($A = \pi r^2$). Use 3.14159 for π, and diameter $\div 2$ for the radius:

$$A = lw - \pi r^2$$
$$A = (30 \text{ meters})(60 \text{ meters}) - 3.14159(15 \text{ meters} \div 2)^2$$
$$A = 1{,}800 \text{ meters}^2 - 3.14159(56.25 \text{ meters}^2)$$
$$A = 1{,}800 \text{ meters}^2 - 176.7 \text{ meters}^2$$
$$A = 1{,}623.3 \text{ meters}^2$$
$$A \approx 1{,}623 \text{ meters}^2$$

9. **A** Lines and Angles

The sum of the two angles must equal 90° since the x-axis and y-axis form sides of the angles. Add the two angles and solve for z:

$$3z + 2z = 90°$$
$$5z = 90°$$
$$z = 18°$$

Find the measure of the two angles by substituting $z = 18°$ into the expression for each angle:

$$3z = 3(18°) = 54°$$
$$2z = 2(18°) = 36°$$

The ACT
Math &
Science
Workbook

10. **K** Circles

The diameter of the circle is equal to the length of the diagonal of the square. You find the length of the diagonal of the square by using the Pythagorean theorem:

Pythagorean theorem	$c^2 = a^2 + b^2$
Substitute, where s = length of the side of the square	$s^2 = 6^2 + 6^2$
Simplify	$s^2 = 36 + 36$
Simplify	$s^2 = 72$
Square root both sides of the equation and simplify	$s = 6\sqrt{2}$

11. **A** Circles

The red circle of fabric must be at least 3 feet from any edge of the white fabric. If you subtract 3 feet from the top of the width and 3 feet from the bottom of the width (which is the smallest dimension), that leaves a maximum of $9 - 3 - 3 = 3$ feet for the diameter of the red circle. The radius is half the diameter, so the red circle can have a maximum radius of 3 feet $\div$ 2 = 1.5 feet. So, **A** is correct.

12. **H** Triangles

This triangle is isosceles because it has two sides that are congruent. In an isosceles triangle, the angles opposite the congruent sides have the same measure. This means that $\angle C$ has the same measure as $\angle B$, which is 35°. The sum of the interior angles of a triangle is 180°, so the measure of $\angle A = 180° - 35° - 35° = 110°$. The correct answer is **H**.

13. **E** Lines and Angles

The measure of $\angle JPQ = 180° - 37° - 63° = 80°$. This is because $\angle KPJ$, $\angle JPQ$, and $\angle QPN$ together form a straight line, which has a measure of 180°. When two lines intersect at one point, the angles formed are called *vertical angles*. Vertical angles are congruent. This means that $\angle MPL \cong \angle JPQ = 80°$, and $\angle NPM \cong \angle KPJ = 37°$. The measure of $\angle LPN$ is equal to the following:

$$\begin{aligned} m\angle LPN &= m\angle MPL + m\angle NPM \\ &= 80° + 37° \\ &= 117° \end{aligned}$$

14. **G** Polygons

The area of the living room in the house is 12 feet × 16 feet = 192 feet². The area is to be tripled. This means the new area will be 3 × 192 feet² = 576 feet². Divide the new area by the new width to find the new length: 576 feet² ÷ (12 feet + 4 feet) = 36 feet. Subtract the old length from the new length to find the increase in the length: 36 feet − 16 feet = 20 feet. The correct answer is **G**.

15. **C** Lines and Angles

When two parallel lines are cut by a transversal $\left(\overline{CD}\right)$, alternate interior angles ($\angle x$ and $\angle 4$) are congruent. Because $\angle 3$ and $\angle 4$ are supplementary, and $\angle 4$ is congruent to $\angle x$, $\angle 3$ is also supplementary to $\angle x$. The correct answer is **C**.

PRACTICE SET 6: TRIGONOMETRY

1. In the right triangle shown below, if $\tan\theta = \dfrac{3}{\sqrt{55}}$, then $\sin\theta = ?$

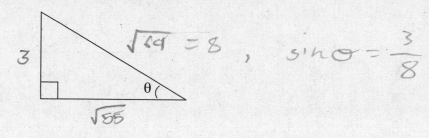

$\sqrt{64} = 8$, $\sin\theta = \dfrac{3}{8}$

A. $\dfrac{3}{8}$

B. $\dfrac{9}{55}$

C. $\dfrac{\sqrt{55}}{8}$

D. $1 - \dfrac{3\sqrt{55}}{55}$

E. $\sqrt{1 - \left(\dfrac{3\sqrt{55}}{55}\right)^2}$

2. In the right triangle shown below, if $\sin\theta = \dfrac{4}{13}$, then $\cos\theta = ?$

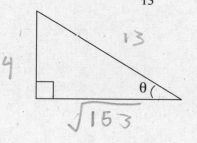

F. $\dfrac{4}{3\sqrt{17}}$

G. $\dfrac{4}{3}$

H. $\dfrac{13}{3\sqrt{17}}$

J. $\dfrac{3\sqrt{17}}{13}$

K. $\dfrac{\sqrt{13}}{4}$

3. In the right triangle shown below, if $\cos\theta = \dfrac{2}{3}$, then $\tan\theta = ?$

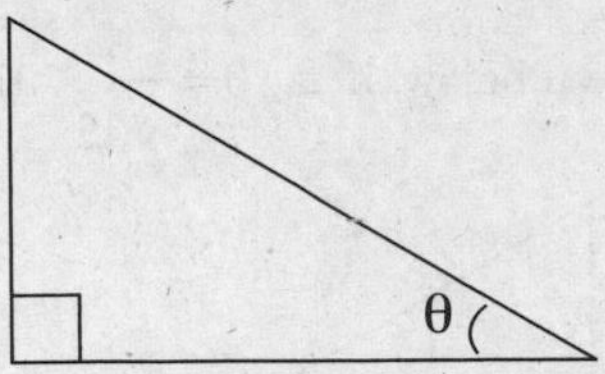

A. $\dfrac{2}{5}$

B. $\dfrac{\sqrt{5}}{2}$

C. $\dfrac{3}{\sqrt{5}}$

D. $\dfrac{5}{2}$

E. $\dfrac{2}{\sqrt{5}}$

4. If $0° \leq \theta° \leq 90°$ and $\sin^2\theta + \cos^2\theta = 1$, what is $\sin\theta$ if $\cos\theta = \dfrac{1}{2}$?

F. $\sqrt{3}$

G. $\dfrac{\sqrt{2}}{2}$

H. $\dfrac{1}{2}$

J. $\dfrac{\sqrt{3}}{2}$

K. $\dfrac{2}{\sqrt{3}}$

5. In the figure below, $\sin \theta = ?$

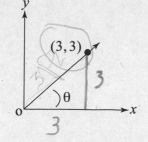

A. $\dfrac{1}{2}$

B. $\dfrac{\sqrt{3}}{2}$

C. $\dfrac{\sqrt{2}}{2}$

D. 1

E. $\sqrt{2}$

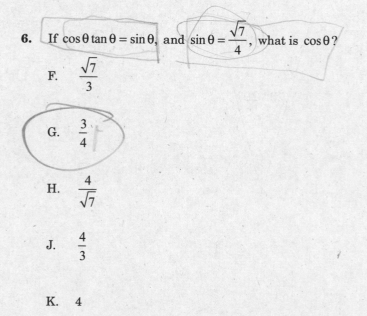

6. If $\cos \theta \tan \theta = \sin \theta$, and $\sin \theta = \dfrac{\sqrt{7}}{4}$, what is $\cos \theta$?

F. $\dfrac{\sqrt{7}}{3}$

G. $\dfrac{3}{4}$

H. $\dfrac{4}{\sqrt{7}}$

J. $\dfrac{4}{3}$

K. 4

7. If $0° \leq \theta° \leq 90°$ and $4\cos^2 \theta - 3 = 0$, then $\theta = ?$
A. $0°$
B. $30°$
C. $45°$
D. $60°$
E. $90°$

$\cos^2 \theta = \dfrac{3}{4}$

$\cos \theta = \pm \dfrac{\sqrt{3}}{2}$

The ACT
Math &
Science
Workbook

8. Whenever $\dfrac{\sin\theta}{\tan\theta}$ is defined, it is equivalent to which of the following?

F. $\cos\theta$

G. $\dfrac{1}{\cos\theta}$

H. $\dfrac{1}{\sin\theta}$

J. $\dfrac{1}{\cos^2\theta}$

K. $\dfrac{\cos\theta}{\sin^2\theta}$

9. A large sail is being sewn for a racing yacht, as shown in the figure below. Which of the following expressions could be used to calculate the height, h, of the sail?

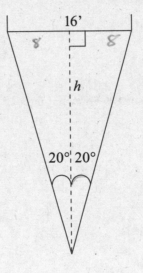

A. $16\tan 20°$

B. $8\tan 40°$

C. $8\tan 20°$

D. $\dfrac{8}{\tan 40°}$

E. $\dfrac{8}{\tan 20°}$

10. From the top of a 15,000-foot peak, the straight line distance ~~to the top of Mount Everest~~ is 14,978 feet. What is the height of Mount Everest if the angle of elevation, θ, from the top of the peak to the top of Mount Everest is 5.074°?

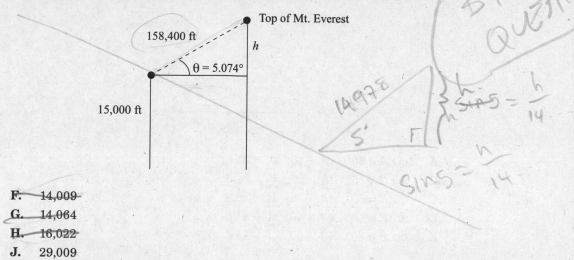

F. ~~14,009~~
G. ~~14,064~~
H. ~~16,022~~
J. 29,009
K. 29,064

11. Solve right triangle ABC if $a = 10.6$ cm and $c = 18.8$ cm. Which of the following are the measures of $\angle A$, $\angle B$, and b?

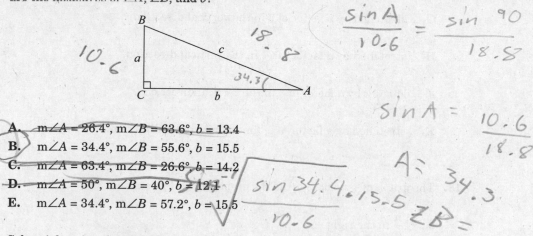

A. m∠A = 26.4°, m∠B = 63.6°, b = 13.4
B. m∠A = 34.4°, m∠B = 55.6°, b = 15.5
C. m∠A = 63.4°, m∠B = 26.6°, b = 14.2
D. m∠A = 50°, m∠B = 40°, b = 12.1
E. m∠A = 34.4°, m∠B = 57.2°, b = 15.5

12. Solve right triangle ABC if $b = 4.8$ m and m∠A = 48°. Which of the following are the measures of $\angle B$, a, and c?

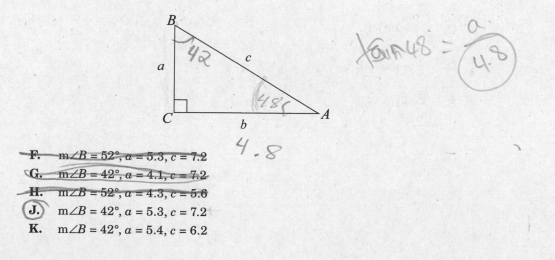

F. m∠B = 52°, a = 5.3, c = 7.2
G. m∠B = 42°, a = 4.1, c = 7.2
H. m∠B = 52°, a = 4.3, c = 5.6
J. m∠B = 42°, a = 5.3, c = 7.2
K. m∠B = 42°, a = 5.4, c = 6.2

13. In $\triangle ACB$ shown below, $\sin A = \dfrac{1}{2}$ and $\overline{BC} = 20$ meters. Which of the following are the measures of $\angle B$, $\overline{AB}$, and $\overline{AC}$?

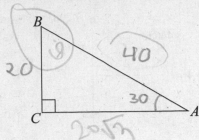

A. $m\angle B = 30°$, $\overline{AB} = 40$, $\overline{AC} = 34.6$
B. $m\angle B = 45°$, $\overline{AB} = 50$, $\overline{AC} = 24.8$
C. $m\angle B = 60°$, $\overline{AB} = 30$, $\overline{AC} = 36.6$
D. $m\angle B = 60°$, $\overline{AB} = 40$, $\overline{AC} = 34.6$
E. $m\angle B = 50°$, $\overline{AB} = 50$, $\overline{AC} = 24.6$

14. The graph of $y = 3 \sin x$ is the graph of $y = \sin x$:

F. shrunk by a factor of $\dfrac{1}{3}$ in the horizontal direction.

G. stretched by a factor of 3 in the vertical direction.

H. stretched by a factor of $\dfrac{1}{3}$ in the vertical direction.

J. shrunk by a factor of 3 in the vertical direction.

K. stretched by a factor of $\dfrac{1}{3}$ in the horizontal direction.

15. The graph of $y = \sin\left(x - \dfrac{\pi}{2}\right)$ is the graph of $y = \sin x$ shifted:

A. $\dfrac{\pi}{2}$ to the right.

B. $\dfrac{\pi}{2}$ to the left.

C. 2 to the left.

D. $\dfrac{1}{2}$ to the left.

E. $\dfrac{1}{2}$ to the right.

PRACTICE SET 6: ANSWERS & EXPLANATIONS

1. **A** ~~SOHCAHTOA~~

You are told that $\tan\theta = \dfrac{3}{\sqrt{55}}$. The tangent of the angle θ is the ratio of the side opposite θ and the side adjacent to θ. This means that the side opposite θ is 3, and the side adjacent to θ is $\sqrt{55}$. See the figure below:

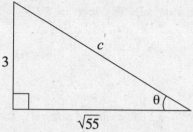

The sine of the angle θ is the ratio of the side opposite θ and the hypotenuse. To find sin θ, you must solve for the length of the hypotenuse, c using the Pythagorean theorem:

Pythagorean theorem	$c^2 = a^2 + b^2$
Substitute	$c^2 = 3^2 + \left(\sqrt{55}\right)^2$
Simplify	$c^2 = 9 + 55$
Simplify	$c^2 = 64$
Take the square root of both sides	$c = 8$

In this problem, the side opposite angle θ is 3 and the hypotenuse is 8, so $\sin\theta = \dfrac{3}{8}$, and the correct answer is **A**.

2. **J** SOHCAHTOA

You are told that $\sin\theta = \dfrac{4}{13}$. The sine of angle θ is the ratio of the side opposite θ and the hypotenuse. This means that the side opposite θ is 4, and the hypotenuse is 13. See the figure below.

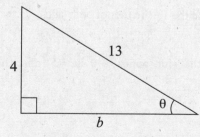

The cosine of angle θ is the ratio of the side adjacent to θ and the hypotenuse. To find cos θ, you must solve for the length of b using the Pythagorean theorem:

Pythagorean theorem	$c^2 = a^2 + b^2$
Substitute	$13^2 = 4^2 + b^2$
Simplify	$169 = 16 + b^2$
Subtract 16 from both sides	$153 = b^2$
Take the square root of both sides	$\sqrt{153} = b$
Factor	$\sqrt{9 \cdot 17} = b$
Simplify	$3\sqrt{17} = b$

In this problem, the side adjacent to θ is $3\sqrt{17}$ and the hypotenuse is 13, so $\cos\theta = \dfrac{3\sqrt{17}}{13}$.

3.   **B**   SOHCAHTOA

You are told that $\cos\theta = \dfrac{2}{3}$. The cosine of angle θ is the ratio of the side adjacent to θ and the hypotenuse. This means that the side adjacent to θ is 2, and the hypotenuse is 3. See the figure below:

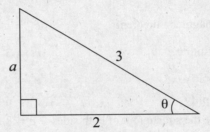

The tangent of the angle θ is the ratio of the side opposite θ and the side adjacent to θ. To find tan θ, you must solve for the length of a using the Pythagorean theorem:

Pythagorean theorem	$c^2 = a^2 + b^2$
Substitute	$3^2 = a^2 + 2^2$
Simplify	$9 = a^2 + 4$
Subtract 4 from both sides	$5 = a^2$
Take the square root of both sides	$\sqrt{5} = a$

In this problem, the side opposite θ is $\sqrt{5}$ and the side adjacent to θ is 2, so $\tan\theta = \dfrac{\sqrt{5}}{2}$.

4. **J** Trigonometric Identities

In this problem, you must substitute $\frac{1}{2}$ for $\cos \theta$ in the equation $\sin^2 \theta + \cos^2 \theta = 1$ and solve for $\sin \theta$:

Trigonometric identity given	$\sin^2 \theta + \cos^2 \theta = 1$
Substitute	$\sin^2 \theta + \left(\dfrac{1}{2}\right)^2 = 1$
Simplify	$\sin^2 \theta + \dfrac{1}{4} = 1$
Subtract $\dfrac{1}{4}$ from each side	$\sin^2 \theta = \dfrac{3}{4}$
Take the square root of both sides	$\sin \theta = \pm \dfrac{\sqrt{3}}{2}$

Since you are given $0° \le \theta° \le 90°$, choose the positive value, since the sine is positive in the first quadrant.

5. **C** SOHCAHTOA

In the figure, you are shown the point (3,3) on the terminal side of angle θ. This means that the two legs of a triangle you could form by dropping a line straight down from that point to the x-axis both have a length of 3.

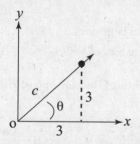

The sine of the angle θ is the ratio of the side opposite θ and the hypotenuse. To find $\sin \theta$, you must solve for the length of the hypotenuse, c, using the Pythagorean theorem:

Pythagorean theorem	$c^2 = a^2 + b^2$
Substitute	$c^2 = 3^2 + 3^2$
Simplify	$c^2 = 9 + 9$
Simplify	$c^2 = 18$
Take the square root of both sides	$c = \sqrt{18}$
Factor	$c = \sqrt{9 \cdot 2}$
Simplify	$c = 3\sqrt{2}$

In this problem, the side opposite is 3 and the hypotenuse is $3\sqrt{2}$, so $\sin \theta = \dfrac{3}{3\sqrt{2}}$.

Now simplify. Divide out the 3s to get $\sin \theta = \dfrac{1}{\sqrt{2}}$. Then rationalize the denominator by multiplying the numerator and denominator by $\sqrt{2}$ and simplifying:

$\sin \theta = \dfrac{\sqrt{2}}{2}$.

The ACT Math & Science Workbook

6. **G** Trigonometric Identities

Solve the identity for cos θ by dividing both sides of the equation by tan θ:

$$\cos\theta\tan\theta = \sin\theta$$

$$\cos\theta = \frac{\sin\theta}{\tan\theta}$$

You are told that $\sin\theta = \dfrac{\sqrt{7}}{4}$. The sin θ is the ratio of the side opposite θ and the hypotenuse. This means the side opposite θ is $\sqrt{7}$ and the hypotenuse is 4.

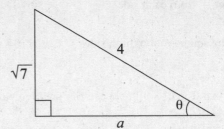

Use the Pythagorean theorem to find the length of a, the side adjacent to θ.

Pythagorean theorem	$c^2 = a^2 + b^2$
Substitute	$4^2 = a^2 + \left(\sqrt{7}\right)^2$
Simplify	$16 = a^2 + 7$
Subtract 7 from both sides	$9 = a^2$
Take the square root of both sides	$3 = a$

The tan θ is equal to the ratio of the side opposite θ and the side adjacent to θ: tan $\theta = \dfrac{\sqrt{7}}{3}$. Now find cos θ:

Write cos θ	$\cos\theta = \dfrac{\sin\theta}{\tan\theta}$
Substitute	$\cos\theta = \dfrac{\dfrac{\sqrt{7}}{4}}{\dfrac{\sqrt{7}}{3}}$
Simplify	$\cos\theta = \dfrac{3}{4}$

7.   **B**   Trigonometric Identities

Solve the identity for $\cos\theta$:

Given identity	$4\cos^2\theta - 3 = 0$
Add 3 to both sides	$4\cos^2\theta = 3$
Divide both sides by 4	$\cos^2\theta = \dfrac{3}{4}$
Take the square root of both sides	$\cos\theta = \dfrac{\sqrt{3}}{2}$

Find θ by taking the inverse cosine of $\dfrac{\sqrt{3}}{2}$: $\cos^{-1}\dfrac{\sqrt{3}}{2} = 30°$. Notice that the answer choices are in degrees, so be sure that your calculator is in degree mode before you take the inverse cosine. The correct answer is **B**.

8.   **F**   Trigonometric Identities

The $\tan\theta$ is equal to $\dfrac{\sin\theta}{\cos\theta}$. Substitute this ratio into the relationship you are given:

Substitute	$\dfrac{\sin\theta}{\tan\theta} = \dfrac{\sin\theta}{\left(\dfrac{\sin\theta}{\cos\theta}\right)}$
Simplify	$\dfrac{\sin\theta}{\tan\theta} = \cos\theta$

9.   **E**   SOHCAHTOA

The length of the side opposite one of the 20° angles is half of 16, or 8. The height is the length of the side adjacent to the 20° angle. You can find h by setting up $\tan 20° = \dfrac{8}{h}$ and solving for h:

$$\tan 20° = \dfrac{8}{h}$$

Multiply both sides by h	$h\tan 20° = 8$
Divide both sides by $\tan 20°$	$h = \dfrac{8}{\tan 20°}$

The correct answer is **E**.

10. **J** SOHCAHTOA

The height of Mount Everest is 15,000 + h. See the figure below.

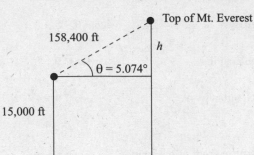

You can find h by setting up the sine function $\left(\dfrac{\text{opposite}}{\text{hypotenuse}}\right)$:

Set up sine function $\qquad\qquad\qquad\qquad \sin\left(5.074°\right)=\dfrac{h}{14{,}978}$

Multiply both sides by 14,978 $\quad 14{,}978\ \sin\left(5.074°\right)=h$

Simplify $\qquad\qquad\qquad\qquad\qquad\qquad 14{,}009=h$

The height of Mount Everest is 15,000 feet + 14,009 feet = 29,009 feet, making **J** the correct answer.

11. **B** Solving Right Triangles

When you solve a right triangle, you must find the measures of the missing angle(s) and side(s). In this problem, you need to find m∠A, m∠B, and length of side b. Find m∠A:

Set up the sine function $\qquad\quad \sin A=\dfrac{a}{c}$

Substitute $\qquad\qquad\qquad\qquad \sin A=\dfrac{10.6}{18.8}$

Simplify $\qquad\qquad\qquad\qquad\ \sin A=0.564$

Set up the inverse function $\qquad A=\sin^{-1}(0.564)$

Simplify $\qquad\qquad\qquad\qquad\ A=34.4°$

You can eliminate **A**, **C**, and **D**. Next, find m∠B:

$$m\angle B = 180° - 90° - 34.4°$$
$$m\angle B = 55.6°$$

Eliminate **E**, which leaves the correct answer **B**. Note: The Pythagorean theorem also could have helped you find b.

12. **J** Solving Right Triangles

When you solve a right triangle, you must find the measures of the missing angle(s) and side(s). In this problem, you need to find m∠B and lengths of sides a and c. Find m∠B:

$$m\angle B = 180° - 90° - 48°$$
$$m\angle B = 42°$$

Eliminate **F** and **H**. Use tan 48° to find a:

Tangent function	$\tan 48° = \dfrac{a}{b}$
Multiply both sides by b	$b \tan 48° = a$
Substitute	$4.8 \tan 48° = a$
Simplify	$5.3 \approx a$

Eliminate **G** and **K**, which leaves only the correct answer **J**. Note: If you would have had to go on and find c, you would have found it using the Pythagorean theorem.

13. **D**   Solving Right Triangles

Given that $\sin A = \dfrac{1}{2}$, you can find A by finding the inverse sine of $\dfrac{1}{2}$:

Sine function you are given	$\sin A = \dfrac{1}{2}$
Set up the inverse sine function	$A = \sin^{-1}\left(\dfrac{1}{2}\right)$
Simplify	$A = 30°$

Find $m\angle B$:

$$m\angle B = 180° - 90° - 30°$$
$$m\angle B = 60°$$

Eliminate **A**, **B**, and **E**. Next, find $\overline{AB}$ using $\sin A = \dfrac{1}{2}$:

Trigonometric function given in the problem	$\sin A = \dfrac{1}{2}$
Substitute the ratio for $\sin A$	$\dfrac{\overline{BC}}{\overline{AB}} = \dfrac{1}{2}$
Substitute 20 for $\overline{BC}$ (given in the problem)	$\dfrac{20}{\overline{AB}} = \dfrac{1}{2}$
Cross multiply	$(1)\left(\overline{AB}\right) = (20)(2)$ $\overline{AB} = 40$

Eliminate **C**, which leaves **D** as the correct answer. Note: The Pythagorean theorem could have helped you find $\overline{AC}$, had the question asked you to do so.

14. **G** Trigonometric Graphs

The coefficient 3 in the equation $y = 3 \sin x$ represents an amplitude of 3 for the graph. The amplitude takes every y-value of the graph of $y = \sin x$ and multiplies it by a factor of 3. This means that every y-value of the graph of $y = \sin x$ is stretched by a factor of 3 in the vertical direction. The correct answer is **G**.

15. **A** Trigonometric Graphs

Adding or subtracting a number from x in the equation $y = \sin x$ shifts the graph left or right by an amount equal to that number. If a number is added, the graph shifts left. If a number is subtracted, the graph shifts right. In the equation you are given, $y = \sin\left(x - \dfrac{\pi}{2}\right)$, $\dfrac{\pi}{2}$ is subtracted from x, so the graph of $y = \sin x$ is shifted a distance of $\dfrac{\pi}{2}$ to the right. The correct answer is **A**.

OVERVIEW OF THE ACT SCIENCE REASONING TEST

The Science Reasoning Test is probably the most feared subject test on the ACT but for the wrong reasons. Time is of the essence on the test: You are given 35 minutes to digest 7 science passages and answer 40 questions on them. But the content of the Science Reasoning Test, which is what usually fills students with trepidation, shouldn't cause you any stress. The term "Science Reasoning" may sound impressive and difficult, but much of the intimidation of the test is mere bluff—big words that disguise simple concepts. In this chapter, you'll learn everything you need to know to unmask and master the ACT Science Reasoning Test.

THE INSTRUCTIONS

You should memorize the instructions for the Science Reasoning Test before you get to the test center. The instructions for this test are pretty straightforward, but you shouldn't even glance at them on test day because time is extremely valuable on the ACT. Read the instructions to yourself a couple times to make sure you have them memorized.

> **DIRECTIONS:** This test contains seven passages, each accompanied by several questions. You should select the answer choice that best answers each question. Within the total allotted time for the test, you may spend as much time as you wish on each individual passage. Calculator use is not permitted.

Don't worry about the last sentence regarding calculator use. There is absolutely no need for a calculator on this test, so it doesn't matter that you're not allowed to use one.

FORMAT OF THE SCIENCE REASONING TEST

The two main components of the Science Reasoning Test are the passages and the questions. We'll briefly explain both below.

The Passages

The Science Reasoning Test has seven science passages:

- 3 Data Representation passages
- 3 Research Summaries passages
- 1 Conflicting Viewpoints passage

Don't be alarmed by the names of the passages, which may sound daunting to you. We'll review each type of science passage and what you'll need to know to succeed on the test. These passages appear in no particular order.

All passages on the Science Reasoning Test will contain data presented in paragraphs, tables, and/or graphs. Each passage will be preceded by a written introduction to, or explanation of, the presented data. There is no standard appearance for the passages, but they all follow the basic principle of providing graphic information in addition to written exposition. The sample passages provided later in this chapter will familiarize you with different possible passage layouts.

The Questions

Each science passage is directly followed by several questions on that passage:

- Data Representation passages are accompanied by 5 questions
- Research Summaries passages have 6 questions
- The Conflicting Viewpoints passage has 7 questions

In the "Content" segment, you'll learn about the types of questions asked. Later in the section, you'll get an in-depth review of how to handle those questions.

CONTENT OF THE SCIENCE REASONING TEST

The "content" of the Science Reasoning Test refers to several kinds of content. First, there are the topics covered by the passages on the test. Second, there are the types of passages on the test. Third, there are the types of questions asked about the different passages. The descriptions below are meant to provide you with brief overviews of each kind of content. Later in the section, we will describe, analyze, and teach you how to handle everything you'll encounter on the Science Reasoning Test.

Passage Topics

The writers of the ACT tell you to expect content covering biology, earth/space sciences, chemistry, and physics on the Science Reasoning passages. That's good advice: The passages on the subject test might discuss data from any of these fields. However, in the end, the Science Reasoning Test doesn't test you on your knowledge of earth sciences or any other field; it tests you on your understanding of scientific data. Where the data comes from—whether it's taken from chemistry or biology experiments—doesn't matter. In other words, *the content is not important*. In this chapter, we'll teach you to ignore the confusing scientific terminology and strike at the heart of the test—the data. But if you're still dying to know about the content of the passages, we'll give you the list below.

- **Biology,** including cell biology, botany, zoology, microbiology, ecology, genetics, and evolution
- **Earth/Space Sciences,** including geology, meteorology, oceanography, astronomy, and environmental sciences
- **Chemistry,** including atomic theory, inorganic chemical reactions, chemical bonding, reaction rates, solutions, equilibriums, gas laws, electrochemistry, organic chemistry, biochemistry, and properties and states of matter

- **Physics,** including mechanics, energy, thermodynamics, electromagnetism, fluids, solids, and light waves

Passage Types

As we've already mentioned, there are three types of science passages on the Science Reasoning Test: Data Representation, Research Summaries, and Conflicting Viewpoints. You will not need to remember the names of the passages for the actual test, but being able to recognize the different passages and knowing what to expect from each will help you greatly. On the practice sets, you will be able to practice with each type of Science Reasoning passage.

Data Representation

The Science Reasoning Test contains three Data Representation passages. These passages contain one or more charts (such as tables, graphs, or illustrations). The accompanying questions test your understanding of and ability to use the information presented in these charts.

Research Summaries

There are three Research Summaries passages on the Science Reasoning Test. These passages generally present two or three related experiments and the data collected from them. You can think of Research Summaries as Data Representation placed in the context of a large experiment.

Conflicting Viewpoints

The test contains only one Conflicting Viewpoints passage. This passage presents you with two or three alternative theories on an observable phenomenon—such as cloud formation or the movement of tectonic plates—and requires that you understand the differences and similarities between the viewpoints.

Question Types

Of the 40 questions on the Science Reasoning Test, 15 will accompany Data Representation passages, 18 will follow Research Summaries, and 7 will cover the Conflicting Viewpoints passage. The four main kinds of questions you'll encounter on the **Data Representation** and **Research Summaries** passages will ask you to:

1. **Read the Chart.** These questions ask you simply to identify information given on the chart and are perhaps the most straightforward questions on the Science Reasoning Test. These questions are the equivalent of Specific Detail questions on the Reading Test.

2. **Use the Chart.** Slightly more complicated than Read the Chart questions, these questions require that you use the information given in the chart to determine other, unstated information. For example, some of these questions might ask you to make an informed guess as to what would happen if one of the variables in an experiment changed.

3. **Handle Graphs.** For these questions, you will either have to translate the information in the charts into words or translate words or numbers into a chart. Being able to manipulate and transform data in this way indicates that you understand exactly what the given information in the passage means.

4. **Take the Next Step.** These questions ask you what the next step should be for research experiments. Generally, this type of question will provide you with a goal for

an experiment and the current scenario. You must decide the next step that should be taken to achieve that goal. You can think of these questions as Big Picture questions that ask you to look at the research or the experiment as a whole.

The questions on the **Conflicting Viewpoints** section are slightly different. We've divided them into three main categories: detail, inference, and comparison.

1. **Detail** questions ask you to identify specific information from the arguments presented.
2. **Inference** questions ask you to draw out implied information from the arguments.
3. **Comparison** questions ask you to find and analyze similarities and differences between the arguments.

STRATEGIES FOR THE SCIENCE REASONING TEST

In many ways, the Science Reasoning Test is similar to a reading test, and, in fact, is very similar to the Reading Test on the ACT. On both of these tests, the questions focus solely on the passages that precede them, so you must understand what you read in order to get the correct answers. As with a reading test, the best (and pretty much the only) way to get correct answers is to understand the passages. For that reason, our strategies are designed to help you with your overall comprehension of the passages—not to provide you with tricks for getting past individual questions.

Don't Be Afraid of the Scientific Jargon

The reason most people seem to be afraid of this test is actually pretty superficial: It's the language. The scientific terminology used on this test can be confusing, but it should not fill you with fear. Underneath the scary language, the Science Reasoning Test is actually quite nice. In fact, once you get past the language, the questions on this test tend to be fairly straightforward and simple to answer.

There are two ways to get past the scientific jargon. The first is simply to know that it *is* jargon. Once you know that the concepts tested by the test are straightforward and merely hidden by a thin veneer of complicated terms, it becomes much easier to see through that jargon. So when you see scientific terminology that seems confusing, don't panic or get nervous. Take a deep breath and break it down. You'll get through it. The second way to defuse scientific jargon is to take practice sets. The more Science Reasoning questions you deal with, the more adept you will be at seeing through the jargon to the straightforward data beneath.

When you read the passage for the first time, you should be reading for a general understanding of it. For Data Representation and Research Summaries passages, look at the provided charts to see which factors or variables are represented. If the passage deals with an experiment, make sure you know what the experiment tests and the goal of the experiment. You should not examine specific aspects of the data, such as how the value of one variable changes against another—leave that sort of analysis for when you answer specific questions.

Remember that there is very little time on this test, so you should not spend a significant amount of time reading the passages. If you labor excruciatingly over every sentence and piece of data in a passage, you will leave yourself little time to answer the questions. You need to find a balance between reading passages and answering questions when you take the practice sets.

Take Notes

If you find that you're having a hard time absorbing the information in the passage, take notes and talk to yourself as you go through it. If a Research Summaries passage has three experiments, say "three experiments" to yourself, or jot it down in the margin, and then note the key differences between the experiments. For example, if each experiment tests a different variable, make sure you know what the variables are.

A few key questions you should ask yourself when reading a science passage are:

- <u>What</u> is being tested?
- <u>Why</u> is it being tested?
- <u>What</u> are the variables?
- What are the factors that stay the same?

[handwritten margin notes: VAR / CTRL / WHY TEST? / WHAT TEST?]

If you ask yourself these questions while reading the passage and make sure you know the answers to them, you will have a leg up when answering the questions.

As you go through the passage asking these questions, jot down your answers in note form next to the relevant sections of the passage. Don't spend too much time making these notes; their main functions are to assist your comprehension of the passage and to jolt your memory when you answer the questions. If you're reading about an experiment that measures acidity, you can scribble "acidity" in the margin by the experiment. If the same experiment varies the concentration of a solution (i.e., if concentration is the variable in the experiment), you can jot down something like: "change conc." You don't have to follow these examples exactly; come up with shorthand expressions that make sense to you. Underlining sentences and circling key information (the variables, for example) will also help you comprehend and remember the passage.

Answer the Questions by Playing a Matching Game

Once you have completed your first reading of the passage and have achieved a solid understanding of what it says, you should move on to the questions. If you come across a question you don't entirely understand, try to restate the question in your own words. Once you know what information the question is looking for, refer back to the passage, using your notes as guidelines.

The most reliable method for choosing the correct answer is essentially playing a matching game. Before looking at the answers, you should try to answer the question *in your own words*. By doing this, you can avoid being influenced by incorrect but tempting answer choices. Once you've come up with your answer, look at the answers provided by the ACT writers and pick the one that best matches your answer. If your answer doesn't match up with any of the choices, you probably did something wrong. In that case, you can quickly go over the question again or move on to the next question, marking the current question so you can come back to it.

Here's a summary of the process for answering questions:

1. Read the question and, if necessary, restate it in your own words so you understand what it is asking.
2. Refer back to the passage.
3. Formulate an answer in your own words, without looking at the answer choices.
4. Match your answer to the choices provided.

Base Your Answers on the Passage

Base your answers only on the contents of the passage. In the case of the Science Reasoning Test, external knowledge has the potential to hurt you. All of the information you need to know is in the passage. You may know more about a subject than the ACT writer designing the questions, but if you read something into a question that the ACT writer didn't intend, you have a good chance of getting the wrong answer.

Remember the Order of Difficulty

As we've emphasized before in this book, knowing the order of difficulty will help determine your overall approach to the test. On the Science Reasoning Test, you can expect to encounter questions roughly in order of increasing difficulty within each passage; however, this order of difficulty does not always hold, and you will sometimes get an easy question at the end of a passage's section. Still, keep this order of increasing difficulty in mind as you answer the questions.

With this handy piece of knowledge, you'll know that you should be able to answer the first questions within a section fairly easily. The first questions usually deal with your comprehension of the information presented in the passage. They tend to be Read the Chart questions in Data Representation and Research Summaries passages and Detail questions in the Conflicting Viewpoints passage. If you cannot answer these questions easily, your understanding of the passage may be fundamentally flawed. In that case, you might want to spend a little time (preferably less than a minute) reviewing the passage to make sure you understand what it means. The practice sets in this workbook will give you practice for each passage type.

REVIEW FOR THE ACT SCIENCE REASONING TEST

Below, we present three sample Science Reasoning passages, one for each type of passage, in the following order: Data Representation, Research Summaries, and Conflicting Viewpoints. We also include explanations and examples of the question types that accompany them.

DATA REPRESENTATION

The three Data Representation passages tend to be the most straightforward passages on the Science Reasoning Test. Each Data Representation passage begins with a written introduction. Read this introduction for a general idea of the passage, but don't labor over it. The charts in Data Representation are the focus of the passage's questions. Use diagrams such as the one below to clarify the often confusing terminology in the introduction and to see graphic representations of the terminology.

Sample Passage

If left at rest, a spring will hang at its equilibrium position. If a mass (M) is attached to that spring, the spring will grow in length by a distance known as its displacement (x). A larger mass will create a larger displacement than a small mass.

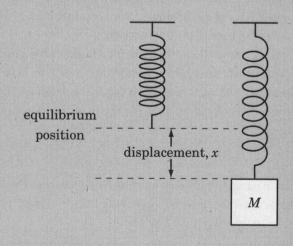

The force (F), in newtons (N), required to return the spring to its equilibrium position is the negative product of the displacement (x) and a spring constant (k), where the negative indicates the direction, not the value, of the force. The spring constant measures the elasticity of a spring: if a spring has a high k, the spring cannot be stretched easily; if a spring has a low k, it can be stretched more easily.

Various masses were attached to two springs with different spring constants, and the force was measured in each of these trials. The energy used (J) returning the spring to its equilibrium position, or Potential Energy (PE), was also measured.

Table 1

Trial	Spring Constant, k	Displacement, x (m)	Force on Spring, F (N)	Potential Energy, PE (J)	Mass, M (g)
1	5	1	5	2.5	M_1
2	5	5	25	62.5	M_2
3	5	10	50	250	M_3
4	10	1	10	5	M_4
5	10	5	50	125	M_5
6	10	10	100	500	M_6

Strategy for Reading the Passage

Since the Data Representation passage is fairly straightforward, you don't necessarily need to employ specific reading strategies. But there are a couple of tips you should keep in mind when going through the passage.

As we suggested, you should read the passage first, and begin by skimming the introduction to the passage. Since the introductions to passages on the Science Reasoning Test are usually full of confusing scientific terminology, you should not spend time struggling to understand everything the introduction says. Rather, use the introduction to get a general idea of what the subsequent chart illustrates. Also, consider circling key terms in the introduction to make referring back to the passage easier.

When you get to the chart (our Data Representation example has only one chart, but you will sometimes come across two), you should glance over it to make sure that you know what's being measured and that, in general, you feel comfortable finding information in the chart. Save detailed exploration of the chart for when you answer specific questions.

The Questions

Each Data Representation passage is accompanied by five questions. These questions fall into one of four categories, and we'll show you how to handle all four below. All of the following questions refer to the sample passage above.

1. **Read the Chart.** These questions test your ability to locate and understand the information presented in the charts provided in the passage. The answers to these questions are usually explicitly stated within the charts. Here's an example of a Read the Chart question:

Which of the following statements about displacement and the force on the spring is consistent with the data in Table 1?

A. The force on the spring increases as displacement increases.
B. The force on the spring decreases as displacement increases.
C. The force on the spring does not change as displacement increases.
D. The force on the spring increases then decreases as displacement increases.

Answering this question is a simple matter of reading the chart. The question explicitly tells you to look at two numbers—the displacement of the spring and the force on the spring—and identify their relationship. All of the answer choices deal with what happens when the displacement increases, so you know that your goal is to see what happens to the force on the spring. Trials 1–3 and Trials 4–6 both show displacement increasing from 1 meter to 5 meters to 10 meters. Your next step should be to check out the corresponding numbers in the Force column. In Trial 1 (a displacement of 1 meter), the force is equal to 5 newtons; in Trial 2 (a displacement of 5 meters), the force is equal to 25 newtons; in Trial 3 (a displacement of 10 meters), the force is equal to 50 newtons. These numbers seem to indicate that force increases with displacement. Now check whether the statement holds true in Trials 4–6. In Trials 4–6, the force rises from 10 newtons to 50 newtons to 100 newtons; in other words, it increases as displacement increases. You've just successfully formulated an answer to the question ("when displacement increases, force increases"), so you can complete the last step of matching your answer with the test's. The correct answer is **A**.

---

2. **Use the Chart.** To answer Use the Chart questions, you must use information from the given chart or charts to decipher additional information. For instance:

According to the information provided in the introduction and Table 1, which of the following is the largest mass?

A. M_1
B. M_3
C. M_5
D. M_6

The question tells you to refer to both the introduction and Table 1. In the introduction, there are two sentences that will help you solve this question. The first sentence is "A larger mass will create a larger displacement than a small mass." This sentence indicates that you should look at the amount of displacement to gauge the relative size of the masses. But if you look only at the displacement, you're probably wondering how to choose between M_3 and M_6, which both indicate a displacement of 10 meters. To solve this problem, look to the crucial sentence found later in the passage: "The spring constant measures the elasticity of a spring: if a spring has a high k, the spring cannot be stretched easily; if a spring has a low k, it can be stretched more easily." This sentence points to the difference between the two springs being tested (one with

$k = 5$ and the other with $k = 10$). If the spring with $k = 10$ is the tougher to stretch of the two, you can assume that it requires a heavier mass to stretch the tough spring 10 meters than it does to stretch the weaker spring 10 meters. So the heaviest mass (and the correct answer) is **D**.

Now try this Use the Chart question:

If Trial 2 were repeated with a spring with $k = 15$, the displacement of the spring would be:

A. less than 5.
B. 5.
C. greater than 5.
D. indeterminable from the given information.

This question resembles the last one in a key way: Both questions require you understand the sentence, "The spring constant measures the elasticity of a spring; if a spring has a high k, the spring cannot be stretched easily; if a spring has a low k, it can be stretched more easily." This sentence tells you that replacing the spring in Trial 2 with a spring that's tougher to pull will result in a smaller displacement of the spring (if the mass pulling on it remains the same). When $k = 5$, Trial 2 produces a displacement of 5 meters, so with a larger k ($k = 15$) and the same mass, the displacement must be less than 5 meters. **A** is correct.

---

3. **Handle Graphs.** These questions will generally ask you to transform the data given in the charts into graphic form. If you are unfamiliar with how to graph data and the differences between linear and exponential functions, you should review this information. Briefly, straight lines indicate linear functions, while curved lines represent exponential functions. Straight horizontal lines indicate that the variable remains constant. For example:

Which of the following graphs best represents the change in potential energy with increasing displacement for Trials 1–3 ?

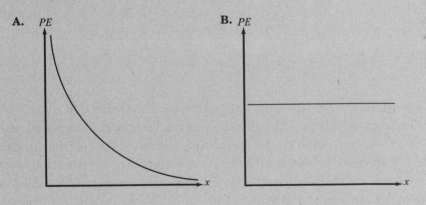

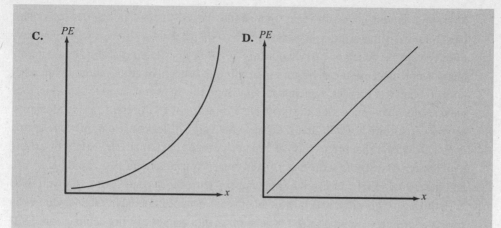

When answering such questions, you should look first at the axes of the graphs. In this question, each of the graphs represents displacement on the *x*-axis, or horizontal axis, while potential energy is represented on the *y*-axis, or vertical axis. As you move right on the *x*-axis and up on the *y*-axis, numerical values increase.

To answer this question, you should first examine the relationship between potential energy and displacement according to Table 1. From the chart, you can see that potential energy rises as displacement increases. Because you're looking for a rise in potential energy, you can eliminate **A** and **B**, since **A** shows potential energy decreasing with an increase in displacement, and **B** shows potential energy remaining constant. Now you've narrowed down your choices to **C** and **D**. The key difference between the graphs of these two choices is that **C** shows potential energy rising exponentially and **D** shows it rising linearly. In other words, the potential energy represented in **C** does not increase in direct proportion to displacement; instead, each incremental increase in displacement leads to an even larger jump in potential energy. From Table 1, you can determine that **C**'s depiction of potential energy is correct because the numbers do not rise in a steady manner (as the numbers for force do).

---

4. **Take the Next Step.** These questions present you with a stated goal that can be achieved through experimentation and tests. Your object is to choose the answer that would best achieve that goal. You will not see these questions as frequently on the Data Representation passages as you will on Research Summaries; in fact, you may not see any of these questions on Data Representation passages, but you should still be prepared to answer them. Here's an example:

What would be the best method of determining how the spring constant affects displacement?

A. Reproduce Trials 1–6 but use only springs with spring constant k = 5.
B. Reproduce Trials 1–3.
C. Reproduce Trials 4–6.
D. Reproduce Trials 1–6 but change the masses in Trials 4–6 to M1, M2, and M3, respectively.

First, you should make sure you understand the goal stated in the question. This particular question wants you to measure how displacement changes when you have different spring constants. Although this question may seem difficult, it is actually fairly simple because it can be answered through process of elimination. If you don't know the answer on your own, just look through the answer choices to see which one makes sense. You know that the goal calls for testing with different spring constants, so you can eliminate **A, B,** and **C** because they all call for the use of just one spring constant. Wasn't that pretty simple? You can double-check that you're right by asking yourself whether **D** makes sense. **D** uses two spring constants ($k = 5$ and $k = 10$), and it proposes that you use the same masses with the second spring that you used with the first. This proposal makes a lot of sense because the only variable will be the spring constant—you won't need to take mass into account in the comparison. So **D** is the correct answer to this problem.

RESEARCH SUMMARIES

For the three Research Summaries passages, you will have to read and understand two or three experiments and their results. The questions accompanying Research Summaries will ask you to compare data across the experiments.

Sample Passage

Brine shrimp, also called *artemia*, are tiny arthropods that are often used as live food in aquariums. The shrimp begin their life cycle as metabolically inactive cysts. The cysts can remain dormant for many years if they relmain dry. If these cysts come in contact with salt water, they soon rehydrate and hatch, giving rise to living embryos.

Experiment 1

Scientists placed dormant brine shrimp cysts into three different soda bottles containing saltwater. The scientists maintained the water in each container at a constant temperature of 25° Celsius (77° Fahrenheit), but they kept the salt concentration (milligrams of NaCl per liter of H_2O) of each bottle at different levels. The scientists then recorded the average hatching rate for the cysts in each bottle.

	Temperature (°C)	Salt Concentration (mg/L)	Average Time to Hatching (hours)
Bottle 1	25	0.2	20
Bottle 2	25	0.3	17
Bottle 3	25	0.4	15

Experiment 2

The scientists repeated Experiment 1, except in this experiment they kept the salt concentration constant while changing the temperature in each bottle.

	Temperature (ºC)	Salt Concentration (mg/L)	Average Time to Hatching (hours)
Bottle 1	15	0.3	33
Bottle 2	25	0.3	17
Bottle 3	35	0.3	26

Experiment 3

The scientists repeated Experiment 1, but placed all three bottles in the dark. The chart below shows the average hatching rate (in hours) for the brine shrimp in the three bottles in Experiment 1 and Experiment 3.

	Experiment 1	Experiment 3
Bottle 1	20	35
Bottle 2	17	28
Bottle 3	15	25

Strategy for Reading the Passage

Earlier, we advised you to take notes while reading the passage. Marginal notes and underlines will particularly help you in reading the Research Summaries passages, which each present you with two or three sets of data.

No matter how carefully you read, you should refer back to the passage when answering the questions. However, if you read too quickly the first time, you run the risk of misunderstanding the basic premise of a passage, and you'll waste time trying to sort out the information when you should be answering the questions.

For this particular passage, jotting down the variables in each experiment in the margins of the passage will help you recall the differences between the experiments. For instance, you might want to write "hatching time" at the top of the passage, so you'll remember that all three experiments test the effect of variables on the hatching time of brine shrimp. Next to Experiment 1, you can write something like "salt conc" to indicate that salt concentration was varied in that experiment. Next to Experiment 2, scribble "temp" to indicate that temperature was the variable. Write "light" or "light vs. dark" next to Experiment 3 to show that the experiment tested hatching time with and without light.

The Questions

Each Research Summaries passage will be followed by six questions. These questions will be similar in type to the questions on the Data Representation passages. All of the questions in this section refer to the sample Research Summaries passage above.

1. **Read the Chart.** As on the Data Representation passage, the Read the Chart questions will ask you to identify information that is explicitly stated in a chart in the passage. For example:

> Based on the results from Experiment 1, one can conclude that:
>
> **A.** brine shrimp hatch less quickly as salt concentration increases.
> **B.** brine shrimp hatch more quickly as salt concentration increases.
> **C.** hatching is unaffected by salt concentration.
> **D.** salt concentration is dependent on temperature.

Since three of the answer choices deal with the hatching of brine shrimp, you should probably look at the column "Average Time to Hatching" and see how the numbers in it change. By reading the chart, you can see that a 0.2 salt concentration corresponds with 20 hours until hatching, a 0.3 salt concentration corresponds with 17 hours until hatching, and a 0.4 salt concentration corresponds with 15 hours until hatching; thus hatching time decreases as salt concentration increases, or brine shrimp hatch *more* quickly as salt concentration increases. **B** seems to be the correct answer. Still, it's good policy to make sure that **C** and **D** do not work before committing to your answer. You can easily eliminate **C**, which states that salt concentration has no effect on hatching time, because Experiment 1 demonstrates the effect of salt concentration on hatching time. Similarly, you can eliminate **D** because it claims that salt concentration depends on temperature. From the chart, you can see that temperature did not vary in Experiment 1, so salt concentration, which did vary, could not have been dependent on it. You've already eliminated **A** by concluding that shrimp hatch more quickly as salt concentration increases, so that leaves you with the correct answer, which is **B**. Here's another Read the Chart question:

> Which of the following was studied in Experiment 3?
>
> **A.** The effect of light on the time it takes for brine shrimp to hatch
> **B.** The effect of light on salt concentration
> **C.** The effect of light on temperature
> **D.** The effect of light on the survival rate of brine shrimp

This question asks you about Experiment 3, and all four answer choices deal with the effect of light on an aspect of the experiment. Your job is to figure out which aspect of the experiment light affects. A quick look at your marginal notes will reveal that Experiment 3 deals with the hatching time of brine shrimp in the dark, using Experiment 1 as a control. You can either look to the chart or its written introduction to find the answer to this question. If you read the introduction, it tells you that the following chart shows the average hatching rate of brine shrimp under the altered circumstances. The chart presents you with no other information, so the experiment must be testing the effect of light on the hatching time of brine shrimp, or **A**.

---

2. **Use the Chart.** Use the Chart questions accompanying Research Summaries passages are very similar to the ones accompanying Data Representation passages. For example:

> If the standard salt concentration used in Experiment 2 were changed from 0.3 mg/L to 0.4 mg/L, what would likely happen to the time it takes for the cysts to hatch?
>
> **F.** The time would increase.
> **G.** The time would decrease.
> **H.** The time would not change.
> **J.** The time would be reduced to zero.

Answering this question requires that you use the charts for both Experiments 1 and 2. As usual, you should see whether you can eliminate one of the answer choices right off the bat. **J** seems like a prime candidate for elimination because neither experiment indicates that the brine shrimp will hatch immediately under any circumstances. To figure out the most likely hatching time, you should look at Experiment 1, which tests changes in salt concentration. The question asks you what would happen if the salt concentration were raised from 0.3 mg/L to 0.4 mg/L. Luckily for you, Experiment 1 tells you what happens to the hatching rate at 0.4 mg/L concentration and 25° temperature: The brine shrimp take 15 hours to hatch. Compare this to the 17 hours it takes for brine shrimp to hatch at 0.3 mg/L and 25°, and you can predict that hatching time will decrease with increased salt concentration. So the best answer for this question is **G**.

Here's a more difficult Use the Chart question:

> Under which of the following conditions would you expect a brine shrimp cyst to hatch in the *least* amount of time?
>
> **A.** In the light, in water with 0.2 mg/L salt concentration at 25 degrees Celsius
> **B.** In the dark, in water with 0.3 mg/L salt concentration at 35 degrees Celsius
> **C.** In the light, in water with 0.4 mg/L salt concentration at 25 degrees Celsius
> **D.** In the dark, in water with 0.2 mg/L salt concentration at 25 degrees Celsius

This question requires that you use all three charts and a little intuition. Some of the answer choices are lifted directly from information in the charts. **A**, for instance, represents Bottle 1 in Experiment 1, with a hatching time of 20 hours. **C**, or Bottle 3 in Experiment 1, has a hatching time of 15 hours. **D**, Bottle 1 in Experiment 3, has a hatching time of 35 hours. **B** is a little trickier than the other answer choices because you must make an educated guess as to its hatching time. The choice states that the bottle is in the dark, so you should keep Experiment 3 in mind. It also states that it has a 0.3 salt concentration and 35° temperature. Since Experiment 1 keeps the temperature constant at 25°, you need to look to Experiment 2, which maintains a 0.3 salt concentration but varies the temperature among 15°, 25°, and 35°. The hatching time for Bottle 3 in Experiment 2, which has the same temperature and salt concentration as **B**, is 26 hours. Since the dark only increases the hatching time for brine shrimp, you can guess that it will take **B** much more than 26 hours to hatch. To keep track of all these hatching times, write down the number of hours for hatching next to each answer choice. The last step in answering the question should be to compare these numbers and choose the smallest one. The correct answer is **C**, with a hatching time of only 15 hours.

---

3. **Handle Graphs.** Questions that ask you to handle graphs on the Research Summaries passage will ask you to transfer information from verbal to graphic form or the other way around. For example:

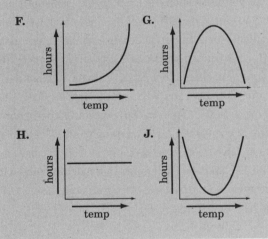

Which of the following graphs best represents the change in hatching time with increasing temperature as shown in Experiment 2?

From the data given with Experiment 2, you can tell that hatching time goes from high to low to high again as temperature increases. These graphs show temperature on the *x*-axis, or horizontal axis, so as you move to the right along the horizontal axis, you are increasing temperature. Similarly, as you move up the *y*-axis, or vertical axis, which represents hatching time, you are increasing the hatching time—33 hours will be higher up on the *y*-axis than 17 hours. Putting all this information together, you should be able to figure out that **J** is correct. If you want proof, you can eliminate the other choices: **F** shows a steadily increasing hatching time; **H** shows a hatching time that doesn't change; and **G** shows a hatching time that goes from small to big to small again, the opposite of what occurs in Experiment 2. Again, review the graphic representations of linear and exponential functions if you are unfamiliar with them.

4. **Take the Next Step.** These questions will be exactly like the Take the Next Step questions on the Data Representation passages. The question will provide you with a new research goal, and you must decide how to achieve it. For example:

> What would be the best way to study the effects of changing pH (acidity) on the hatching time of brine shrimp cysts?
>
> A. Putting all three bottles in the light and keeping temperature constant while changing salt concentration and pH
> B. Putting all three bottles in the dark and keeping temperature constant while changing salt concentration and pH
> C. Putting all three bottles in the light and keeping temperature and salt concentration levels constant while varying the pH in each bottle
> D. Putting all three bottles in the dark and varying temperature, salt concentration, and pH in all three bottles

This question asks you to make pH the variable in the new experiment. Since pH is the variable in this new experiment, you want to keep the other factors as constant and as "normal" as possible. But **A**, **B**, and **D** all ask you to change other factors, such as salt concentration or temperature. These modifications would make it tough to tell whether a change in hatching time was caused by a change in pH levels or by one of the other variables, and that defeats the goal of the experiment. **C**, the only choice that keeps light, salt concentration, and temperature constant, is the correct answer.

CONFLICTING VIEWPOINTS

As we briefly mentioned earlier in this chapter, the Conflicting Viewpoints passage in many ways resembles the Reading Test passages. Because of this resemblance, we advise you to divorce the Conflicting Viewpoints passage from the Science Reasoning Test in your mind and to think of it as a misplaced Reading Test passage. The new slant on this passage should affect your approach to the passage and (for most people) should make it seem less intimidating.

Sample Passage

> The theory of plate tectonics, which describes the shifting of the Earth's plates (most of which contain pieces of continents), is now widely accepted as correct. But scientists are still debating the driving mechanism behind plate tectonics; in other words, they want to know how the shifting of plates happens. Two of the most popular hypotheses for explaining this phenomenon are presented to you below.

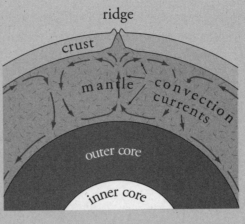

Figure 1a

Mantle Convection Theory

Proponents of this theory argue that tectonic plates are moved passively by convection currents in the Earth's mantle, which is the layer below the crust. Mantle rocks near the Earth's core become extremely hot, making them less dense than the cooler mantle rocks in the upper layers. As a result, the hot rocks rise and the (relatively) cool rocks sink, creating slow vertical convection currents within the mantle (see Figure 1a). These convection currents in turn create convection cells, pockets of circulation within the mantle. Supporters of the mantle convection theory argue that these convection cells directly cause documented seafloor spreading, which they claim is responsible for plate movement. The convection currents push up magma, forming new crust and exerting a lateral force on the plate, pushing it apart and "spreading" the seafloor (see Figure 1b). The scientists claim that this force, which ultimately results from convection currents, is the driving force behind the movement of tectonic plates.

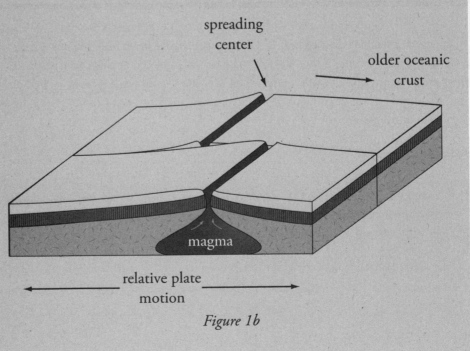

Figure 1b

Slab Pull Theory

This theory posits that gravity and the plates themselves are responsible for tectonic plate movement through a process known as subduction. Subduction zones exist at the outer edges of plates where the rock is cool and dense (as rock ages, it cools off and becomes increasingly dense) (see Figure 2a). In these zones, the old rock is so dense that it subducts, or sinks, into the mantle below it, pulled down by gravitational forces. As the slab (the subducting part of the plate) is pulled down into the mantle, it drags the rest of the plate along with it, causing tectonic plate movement (see Figure 2b). The density of the slab will affect the velocity of its subduction and thus the force it applies on the plate; a very dense slab will sink faster than a less dense slab because of gravitational pull, and it will exert a greater force on the plate attached to it. This theory explains mantle convection as a product, rather than a cause, of plate movement. The outward movement of the plate allows hot magma to bubble up from the Earth's mantle at the center ridges of the plate, forming new crust where the older crust used to be.

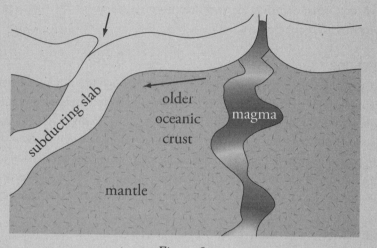

Figure 2a

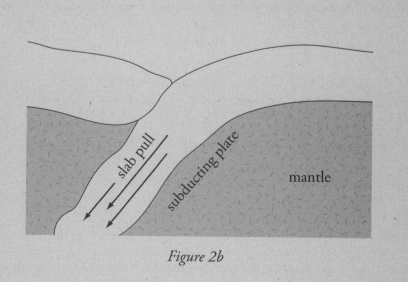

Figure 2b

Strategy for Reading the Passage

Because the questions accompanying this passage almost exclusively deal with the written material in the passage, it is particularly important that you have a strong grasp of what the passage says and that you can refer back to the passage efficiently. For that reason, you should underline and circle sentences and phrases that could potentially be important for answering questions. These underlines and circles will guide you through the passage when you refer back to it. Also try to get an overall sense of what each passage is arguing and the most important ways in which the two arguments differ.

The heavy use of scientific terms makes this passage difficult to digest. Mantle rocks, convection currents, subduction—what does it all mean? The figures at the end illustrate these terms, but you may still feel confused. Don't let the confusion bother you. You don't need to understand convection currents after reading this passage. Take from the passage only what it gives you: a brief explanation of the formation of convection currents and their role in the process described. As long as you understand that convection currents are related to the rise of hot rocks and the fall of cooler, denser rocks; that convection currents form convection cells; and that the two theories disagree about the cause and effect of convection currents, you're all set.

The Questions

The seven questions on the Conflicting Viewpoints passage are different from the other questions in the Science Reasoning Test. They break down into only three categories: Detail, Inference, and Comparison. There may be questions for which you can immediately eliminate one of the answer choices, but elimination will not be your standard technique for solving problems. Rather, you must develop good reading comprehension skills, since Conflicting Viewpoints is fundamentally a reading comprehension passage. All of the example questions in this section refer to the Conflicting Viewpoints passage above.

---

1. **Detail.** There will probably be two Detail questions on the Conflicting Viewpoints passage. Detail questions ask you for specific information from the passage. They address only one viewpoint at a time and usually deal with a key aspect of that viewpoint. To answer these questions, you need a fundamental grasp of what each side is arguing.

   Try this Detail question:

   According to the Mantle Convection Theory, the heating of mantle rocks near the Earth's core directly results in:

   A. the rising of the rocks to the upper mantle because they become buoyant when hot.
   B. the spreading of the seafloor as magma pushes up through the crust.
   C. the creation of convection cells within the mantle.
   D. the subduction of cool plate edges into the less dense mantle.

   A key word in this question is *directly* because it indicates that the answer should be a direct and *immediate* result of the heating of mantle rocks. While the heating of the rocks may eventually lead to more than one of the answer choices, only one answer choice directly results from it. If you run down through the choices, you will see that **D** discusses subduction, which is mentioned exclusively in the Slab Pull Theory; thus you can eliminate **D** because it is irrelevant to the Mantle Convection Theory. Elimination helps you on this sort of question, but, as in the case of this particular question, it might not bring you all the way to the correct answer. Now refer back to the passage and find the section on the heating of mantle rocks. Without spending much time rereading the section, recall the sequence of events (any marks you made will help you here), and then formulate an answer to the question. The correct answer to this question is **A** because the rising is the immediate result of the heating of the mantle rocks. According to the Mantle Convection Theory, **B** and **C** result from heated mantle rocks, but they occur later in the sequence of events.

Now try this Detail question on the Slab Pull Theory:

According to the Slab Pull Theory, which of the following is NOT true?

A. Subduction zones exist far from the active central ridges of plates.
B. Tectonic plate movement results from a lateral force caused by subduction.
C. Mantle convection occurs independently of subduction.
D. Gravitational forces act on dense slab.

This question differs from the previous one because it asks you to identify the answer choice that is *false* according to the Slab Pull Theory. Because of the question's phrasing, you will not be able to come up with your own answer before matching it to the answer choices. Instead, you should make sure you understand the theory and refer back to the passage when necessary, keeping in mind that the time you spend on this step should be limited. Once you feel comfortable with the passage, run down through the answer choices and ask yourself whether you found each one in the passage. If you understood the main point of the Slab Pull Theory, **C** should jump out at you because it describes something occurring *independently* of subduction, while the Slab Pull Theory depends on subduction. Indeed, **C** is the correct answer to this question.

2. **Inference.** You will probably see two Inference questions on the Conflicting Viewpoints passage. These questions ask you to make inferences (i.e., figure out implied information) based on the arguments of each viewpoint.

Sometimes Inference questions will present you with a hypothetical situation and ask you how the proponents of one (and sometimes both) of the viewpoints would react to it. For instance:

If it were discovered that slabs break off from the rest of the plates once a certain degree of force is applied, the discovery would harm:

A. the Mantle Convection Theory.
B. the Slab Pull Theory.
C. both theories.
D. neither theory.

This question asks you to decide what the consequences of this discovery would be. The terms used in this question will help get you started. The question discusses slabs and gravitational forces, which should immediately point you in the direction of the Slab Pull Theory. Your next step should be to consider how the new evidence affects the Slab Pull Theory. Ask yourself, "What does the theory say?" Well, the Slab Pull Theory maintains that subducting slabs exert a pull on the plates to which they're attached. If the new evidence is correct and the slabs break off from the plate when too much force is applied, the new evidence is harmful to the Slab Pull Theory, and **B** is the correct answer.

Inference questions may also ask you to identify a statement or piece of evidence that lends support to one of the viewpoints. For example:

Scientists decide to observe the outer edges of plates. Which of the following statements about subduction zones would support the Slab Pull Theory?

A. Not all plates have subduction zones.
B. Slab subducts at a uniform speed in all subduction zones.
C. Slab subducts at various speeds depending on the age of the slab.
D. Where oceanic plates meet continental plates, the oceanic plates will subduct because they are more dense than continental plates.

Answering this question will require the same skills you used to answer the previous question, but here you have to figure out the consequences of four different discoveries instead of just one. Because this task is potentially time-consuming, you should first run down the answer choices to see whether you can instantly eliminate any as either absolutely incorrect or simply irrelevant to the Slab Pull Theory. Going through this particular set, you may choose to eliminate **A** and **D** right away. If scientists declared that **A** were true, they would definitely not be supporting the Slab Pull Theory, as the theory hinges on the widespread existence of subduction zones. **D**, you might decide, is irrelevant to the theory because the theory never mentions oceanic or continental plates. So you are left with two choices: **B** and **C**. Interestingly, they both deal with the speed at which plates subduct. Does either the Slab Pull Theory or the Mantle Convection Theory talk about speed? According to the Slab Pull Theory, "the density of the slab will affect the velocity of its subduction [and] a very dense slab will sink faster than a less dense slab." In other words, the Slab Pull Theory expects the velocity (or speed) of subduction to vary depending on the density of the slab. **C** says that slabs subduct at different speeds depending on the *age* of the slab, so can it still be the correct answer? Yes, because the summary of the Slab Pull Theory also tells you that the older the rock is, the denser it will be. So **C** would support the Slab Pull Theory.

You may encounter other types of Inference questions on the test. For instance, an Inference question might ask you to identify a necessary assumption made by one of the viewpoints, but you shouldn't panic if you see a question like that. All Inference questions, regardless of their phrasing, can be handled similarly. As with Detail questions, getting Inference questions right on this test depends almost entirely on your ability to comprehend and use the information provided in the passage.

3. **Comparison.** These questions generally account for three of the seven questions accompanying the Conflicting Viewpoints passage, so you should make sure you feel comfortable with them. They require you to compare the viewpoints in the passage in terms of specific details presented in each argument or inferences you must draw about the viewpoints.

Comparison questions frequently ask you to identify points on which the viewpoints would agree or disagree. For example:

About which of the following points do the two theories differ?

A. Movement of tectonic plates across the Earth's surface
B. Density of hot mantle rocks
C. Existence of convection currents in the Earth's mantle
D. Role of mantle convection in tectonic plate movement

This question requires that you use both your ability to compare viewpoints and your ability to identify specific detail; answering it correctly involves no inference work. To start, you should read through the answer choices, eliminating anything you know is uncontroversial to the viewpoints. **A**, for instance, is uncontroversial because both of the viewpoints acknowledge that the plates move; in fact, their goal is to explain this movement. (The theories disagree on the mechanism behind this movement, not on the movement itself.) Ideally, you should be able to get the right answer to this question without referring back to the passage, as this question deals with the fundamental difference between the two theories. If you can't answer this question on your own, you should refer back to the passage quickly, but do not waste a lot of time reading through it again. The correct answer to this problem is **D**. The Mantle Convection Theory argues that mantle convection is the driving force behind plate movement, while the Slab Pull Theory maintains that mantle convection merely results from plate movement. **B** is wrong because only the Slab Pull Theory deals with the density of mantle rocks, and **C** is wrong because neither theory denies the existence of convection currents.

Comparison questions may also ask you to infer how one theory would address the other. For instance:

How would supporters of the Slab Pull Theory explain the documentation of seafloor spreading cited in the Mantle Convection Theory?

A. Seafloor spreading directly causes tectonic plate movement and slab subduction.
B. Seafloor spreading does not exist.
C. Seafloor spreading and slab subduction simultaneously exert moving forces on tectonic plates.
D. Seafloor spreading exists, but only as a result of slab subduction.

You could call this an inference-comparison question because it asks you to figure out something that is not explicitly stated in the passage: the response of one theory to the other. The question points you to a specific issue under debate: seafloor spreading. Ask yourself whether you understand the position of the Slab Pull Theory on seafloor spreading. The passage explicitly states that Slab Pull theorists consider mantle convection and seafloor spreading to be products, not causes, of slab subduction. Which of the answer choices captures that position? **A** says that seafloor spreading directly causes slab subduction (the opposite of what the Slab Pull Theory says), so it is incorrect. **B** is also incorrect because the Slab Pull Theory does not deny that the seafloor spreads. **C** is incorrect as well because it says that both seafloor spreading and slab subduction are responsible for plate movement, whereas the Slab Pull Theory argues that only slab subduction is responsible. **D**, then, must be correct, but you should always double-check. In accordance with the Slab Pull Theory, it says that seafloor spreading is a result of slab subduction, so **D** is indeed the correct answer to the question.

You may encounter additional types of Comparison questions on the actual ACT, but they will all follow the basic idea of comparing the presented arguments in terms of specific details or inferences. If you encounter a Comparison question that seems unlike the examples given above, the difference is usually a matter of phrasing. A Comparison question worded, "Which of the following statements about the factors that affect tectonic plate movement would be consistent with the Mantle Convection and Slab Pull theories?" really just asks you to identify specific details from both theories that agree. You shouldn't have any problem with this question if you understand how to answer the first example in this section.

If you get a Conflicting Viewpoints passage that presents three arguments, you may see other variations on the types of questions asked. For instance, a question may ask you to identify how one theory is better than the other two in a specific regard. That question would also be a detail-comparison question because it asks you about a specific aspect addressed by the three arguments. Again, you won't have a problem if you understand the examples above.

The key to avoid being intimidated by Comparison questions is to remember that they are Detail and Inference questions that simply deal with multiple viewpoints. If you can answer Detail and Inference questions, you're well on your way to mastering Comparison questions as well.

PRACTICE FOR THE ACT SCIENCE REASONING TEST

SCIENCE TEST

35 Minutes—40 Questions

DIRECTIONS: This test contains seven passages, each accompanied by several questions. You should select the answer choice that best answers each question. Within the total allotted time for the test, you may spend as much time as you wish on each individual passage. Calculator use is not permitted.

PRACTICE SET 1: DATA REPRESENTATION

Passage I

Citation: Olthof MR, Bots ML, Katan MB, Verhoef P (2006) Effect of folic acid and betaine supplementation on flow-mediated dilation: A randomized, controlled study in healthy volunteers. PLoS Clin Trials 1(2): c10. DOI: *10.1371/journal.pctr.0010010*

Scientific evidence suggests that high concentrations of homocysteine (an amino acid) in the blood may increase an individual's risk of cardiovascular disease. However, the basis for the link between homocysteine and cardiovascular disease risk is not clear. A trial was conducted to further investigate whether lowering homocysteine levels lowers heart disease risk. The trial was performed on 40 healthy men and women, aged 50–70 years. Table 1 shows characteristics of the participants at the start of the study.

Table 1	
Characteristic	**Mean**
Age	59 years
Systolic blood pressure	130 mmHg
Diastolic blood pressure	74 mmHg
Total homocysteine	12.0 µmol/l
Folate	16.8 nmol/l
Vitamin B_{12}	347 pmol/l
Vitamin B_6	77.1 nmol/l
Total cholesterol	5.8 mmol/l

Homocysteine levels can be lowered by supplementing the diet with B-vitamins, such as folic acid. In the study, volunteer participants were given either folic acid supplementation, a placebo, or betaine, another nutrient that lowers homocysteine levels. (A placebo is essentially a "blank" that contains no supplementation, but participants are not told that they are receiving the placebo.) Each participant in the trial received all three treatments for six weeks each, with a six-week waiting period before the next treatment was given. Table 2 shows the results.

Table 2			
	Mean		
Outcome Measure	Placebo	Folic Acid	Betaine
Total homocysteine (µmol/l)	9.9	8.0	8.7
Folate (nmol/l)	16.1	53.0	14.4

Vascular function is a marker for risk of cardiovascular disease. The researchers used a technique called flow-mediated dilation (FMD) to measure functioning of the main artery of the upper arm in each subject. Increases in FMD% reflect increases in vascular functioning. Figure 1 shows the results. Each spot represents the average FMD measurement at the end of the treatment period for one participant. Each line represents the average FMD measurement for all participants for each treatment type.

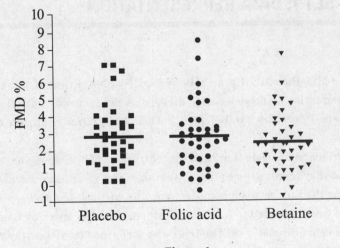

Figure 1

1. According to Figure 1, by how many percentage points does the FMD% of patients treated with folic acid differ from that of patients treated with the placebo?

   A. 0
   B. 1
   C. 2
   D. 3

2. According to Tables 1 and 2, patients treated with folic acid saw a reduction in homocysteine levels of:

F. 2.1 µmol/l
G. 3.3 µmol/l
H. 4.0 µmol/l
J. 8.8 µmol/l

3. Which of the following is associated with decreased levels of folate in the study subjects?

A. Supplementation with folic acid
B. Administering of vitamin B_6
C. Supplementation with betaine
D. Total homocysteine levels

4. According to Figure 1, how do the FMD levels of patients treated with folic acid correspond to the FMD levels of patients treated with betaine?

F. The mean FMD levels of patients treated with folic acid are nearly twice those of patients treated with betaine.
G. One of the patients treated with folic acid had a higher FMD level than any of the patients treated with betaine.
H. Nearly all of the patients treated with betaine had significantly lower FMD levels than the patients treated with folic acid.
J. The mean FMD levels of patients treated with folic acid were lower than the mean FMD levels of patients treated with betaine.

5. Based on the information in the passage and the tables, which of the following statements best describes the relationship between betaine, folic acid, and cardiovascular disease risk?

A. Both betaine supplementation and folic acid supplementation significantly decrease the risk of cardiovascular disease.
B. Folic acid supplementation significantly decreases the risk of cardiovascular disease, but betaine supplementation does not.
C. Betaine supplementation significantly decreases the risk of cardiovascular disease, but folic acid supplementation does not.
D. Neither betaine supplementation nor folic acid supplementation significantly decreases the risk of cardiovascular disease.

PRACTICE SET 1: ANSWERS & EXPLANATIONS

1. **A** Read the Chart
    Figure 1 shows that patients treated with folic acid had FMD measurements of approximately 3%. Patients treated with the placebo also had FMD measurements of 3%. The measurements are the same, so their difference is zero. The correct answer is **A**.

2. **H** Use the Chart
    Before the study, the average homocysteine reading of the subjects was 12.0 µmol/l. Afterward, patients treated with folic acid had homocysteine readings 8.0 µmol/l, which represents a decrease of 4.0 µmol/l. **H** is therefore correct. **F** represents the decrease in patients treated with the placebo, and **G** represents the decrease in patients treated with betaine.

3. **C** Use the Chart
    At the start of the study, the average folate level of the subjects was 16.8 nmol/l. After the study, patients treated with betaine had lower folate levels (14.4 nmol/l). Patients treated with folic acid had higher folate levels (53.0 nmol/l), so **A** is incorrect. The best choice is **C**.

4. **G** Use the Chart
    In Figure 1, the readings for the betaine and folic acid groups are very similar, so **F** and **H** are incorrect. **J** reflects the opposite of what Figure 1 shows: FMD levels for the betaine group were the lowest of all, by a very slight amount. However, the highest FMD reading (more than 8%) was recorded for an individual in the folic acid group. This individual had a higher FMD reading than any of the patients in the betaine group. So, **G** is correct.

5. **D** Use the Chart
    Table 2 shows that both folic acid and betaine supplementation significantly lowered homocysteine levels in study subjects. However, neither form of supplementation produced any significant change in vascular function, as measured using FMD. Figure 1 shows that both folic acid and betaine levels had nearly the same effect on FMD levels, as did the placebo. In other words, they produced the same results as the "no treatment option," failing to lower FMD levels. Neither folic acid nor betaine decreased the risk of cardiovascular disease, so eliminate **A**, **B**, and **C**. The correct answer is **D**.

PRACTICE SET 2: DATA REPRESENTATION

Passage II

Citation: Hoag, D. L.; Popp, J. S. H.; Hyatt, D. E. (1998) Sustainability and resource assessment: a case study of soil resources in the United States. Research Triangle Park, NC: U.S. Environmental Protection Agency, Office of Research and Development; report no. *EPA/600/R-98/038.*

Figure 1 shows the quality of three different types of soil.

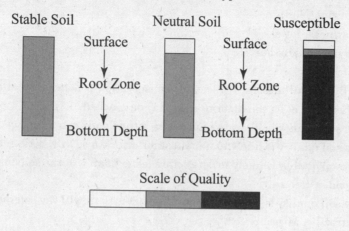

Figure 1

Different types of soil deteriorate at different rates. The rate of deterioration is affected by conservation practices. Figure 2 shows the paths of soil quality deterioration for three different types of soil. The solid line shows soil deterioration when no conservation practices are applied. The dotted line shows soil deterioration when conservation practices are applied.

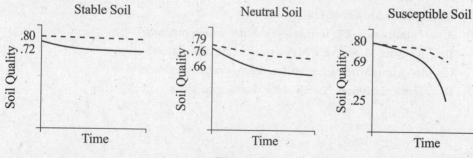

Figure 2

Table 1 shows the soil types of three different regions in the states of Iowa, Missouri, and Minnesota.

Table 1			
	Soil Type		
Region	**Stable**	**Neutral**	**Susceptible**
Iowa	Tama	Dinsdale	Nordness
Missouri	Haymond	Mexico	Hartville
Minnesota	Port Byron	Kenyon	Rockton

1. According to the passage, over time, the soil that will deteriorate most quickly is:

    A. susceptible soil without conservation practices.
    B. neutral soil without conservation practices.
    C. stable soil with conservation practices.
    D. susceptible soil with conservation practices.

2. According to the information presented in Figure 1 and Table 1, which of the following locations has the poorest soil quality?

    F. Kenyon, Minnesota
    G. Dinsdale, Iowa
    H. Nordness, Iowa
    J. Haymond, Missouri

3. If Port Byron, Minnesota, implements conservation practices, what conclusion about the speed of its soil deterioration may be reached?

    A. Its soil quality is likely to improve for a time and then abruptly decrease.
    B. Its soil quality is likely to remain stable over time, with little deterioration.
    C. Its soil quality is likely to deteriorate faster than will the soil quality of Haymond, Missouri.
    D. Its soil quality is likely to deteriorate faster than will the soil quality of Hartville, Missouri.

4. According to Figure 1, all soil types possess which of the following?

    F. Medium quality soil at their root zones
    G. High quality soil at their root zones
    H. Poor quality soil at their bottom depths
    J. High quality soil on their surface layers

5. According to the information presented in Figure 2 and Table 1, the slowest rate of soil deterioration will be found in:

    A. Tama, Iowa, if it implements conservation practices.
    B. Kenyon, Missouri, with no conservation practices.
    C. Rockton, Minnesota, with no conservation practices.
    D. Mexico, Missouri, with conservation practices.

PRACTICE SET 2: ANSWERS & EXPLANATIONS

1.   **A**   Read the Chart
Figure 2 shows soil deterioration over time. The slope of the line on the graph indicates the speed of soil deterioration: The steeper the downward slope, the faster the deterioration. The solid black line in Figure 2 reflects soil deterioration when no conservation practices are applied. For susceptible soil, the solid line drops off to the right more quickly than any other line in Figure 2, so **A** is correct. **C** represents the soil that will deteriorate least quickly. For stable soil, the dotted line represents conservation practices. This line does not drop off to the right at all, so **C** is incorrect.

2.   **H**   Use the Chart
Figure 1 shows that susceptible soil has the greatest percentage of poor quality soil. Table 1 shows that Nordness, Iowa, has susceptible soil. The remaining locations among the answer choices have either neutral soil, **F** and **G**, or stable soil, **J**. So, the correct answer is **H**.

3.   **B**   Use the Chart
According to Table 1, Port Byron has stable soil. Figure 2 shows that stable soil doesn't deteriorate much over time. With conservation practices, the quality of stable soil can be expected to remain constant. Eliminate **A**, **C**, and **D** because with conservation practices, the soil in Port Byron isn't likely to deteriorate. The correct answer is **B**.

4.   **J**   Read the Chart
Figure 1 shows that all soil types have a surface layer with high quality soil. **J** is therefore correct. **F** and **H** are wrong because stable soil is high quality at all levels. **G** is wrong because only stable soil is high quality in the root zone.

5.   **A**   Use the Chart
Figure 2 shows that the slowest soil deterioration occurs in areas with stable soil and conservation practices. Table 1 shows that Tama, Iowa, has stable soil. The correct answer is **A**. **B** and **C** are incorrect because Kenyon and Rockton have neutral and susceptible soil, respectively. With no conservation practices, the soil in these areas would deteriorate faster than the stable soil in Tama, Iowa. **D** is also wrong because Table 1 shows that Mexico, Missouri, has neutral soil. According to Figure 2, neutral soil with conservation practices would deteriorate more quickly than stable soil with conservation practices.

PRACTICE SET 3: DATA REPRESENTATION

Passage III

Citation: Levy JI, Baxter LK, Katan MB, Clougherty JE (2006) The air quality impacts of road closures associated with the 2004 Democratic National Convention in Boston. *Environmental Health: A Global Access Science Source* 5(16). DOI: *10.1186/1476-069X-5-16*

During the Democratic National Convention in 2004, the city of Boston closed multiple roads. Traffic patterns were measured before, during, and after the convention. Figure 1 shows the number of vehicles per hour on highways that had road closures during the convention. The solid line represents traffic averages in the weeks before and after the convention. The dotted line represents traffic during the convention. Time of day is indicated in hours across the x-axis.

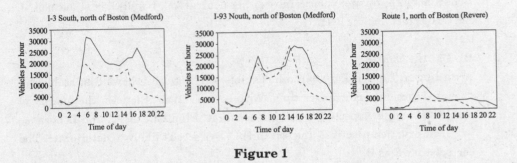

Figure 1

Figure 2 shows the number of vehicles per hour on highways that did not have road closures during the convention. The solid line represents traffic averages in the weeks before and after the convention. The dotted line represents traffic during the convention. Time of day is indicated in hours across the x-axis.

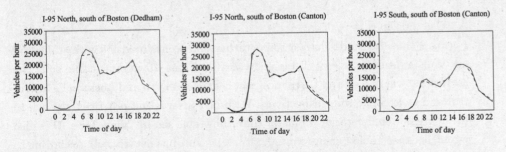

Figure 2

To determine the effect of road closures on air pollution, nitrogen dioxide (NO_2) concentrations were measured at various sites. Table 1 shows the relationship between road closures and NO_2 levels. The third column represents an average of readings taken in the weeks before and after the convention, when there were no road closures.

Table 1		
Site Type	Median NO_2 concentration (ppb) during road closures	Median NO_2 concentration (ppb) before and after road closures
Type 1 – Sites near a closed-down road, with no alternate routes	7 ppb	10 ppb
Type 2 – Sites near an alternate route but not a closed-down road	14 ppb	12 ppb
Type 3 – Sites isolated from road closures or alternate routes	11 ppb	12 ppb

1. According to Figure 1, traffic on I-93 North experienced the greatest reduction due to road closures between the hours of:
   A. 14:00 and 22:00.
   B. 8:00 and 14:00.
   C. 0:00 and 2:00.
   D. 2:00 and 8:00.

2. It was hypothesized that NO_2 emissions would be reduced during road closures at monitoring sites located near a closed-down road with no nearby alternative routes. Was this hypothesis supported by the results provided in Table 1?
   F. No, because before and after the road closures, Type 3 sites had increased NO_2 emissions compared to convention traffic.
   G. No, because before and after the road closures, Type 1 sites had decreased NO_2 emissions compared to convention traffic.
   H. Yes, because during the road closures, Type 1 sites had decreased NO_2 emissions compared to non-convention traffic.
   J. Yes, because during the road closures, Type 2 sites had increased NO_2 emissions compared to non-convention traffic.

3. If one were to compare the convention traffic patterns to non-convention patterns at each site shown in Figure 2, one would conclude that the differences in the traffic patterns were:
   A. greatest for I-95 South and smallest for I-95 North in Dedham.
   B. greatest for I-95 South and smallest for I-95 North in Canton.
   C. relatively minimal over all three traffic sites at all hours.
   D. minimal for all three sites during the daytime hours only.

4. One of the site types in the study was hypothesized to reflect an increase in NO_2 emissions during the week of the convention. Does the information in Table 1 provide data that supports this hypothesis?
   F. Yes, because Type 3 sites reflected an increase in NO_2 levels of 1 ppb during road closures.
   G. Yes, because Type 2 sites reflected an increase in NO_2 levels of 2 ppb during road closures.
   H. No, because Type 3 sites reflected a decrease in NO_2 levels of 1 ppb during road closures.
   J. No, because Type 2 sites reflected a decrease in NO_2 levels of 2 ppb during road closures.

5. If lower volumes of traffic lead to decreased NO_2 emissions, which of the highways in Figures 1 and 2 is most likely to represent a Type 1 site from Table 1?

    A. I-95 South

    B. I-95 North (Dedham)

    C. I-95 North (Canton)

    D. I-93 South

PRACTICE SET 3: ANSWERS & EXPLANATIONS

1.   **A**   Read the Chart

Traffic on I-93 North is represented on the middle graph. The solid line represents traffic before and after the convention, when roads were open. The dotted line represents traffic during the convention, when roads were closed. The gap between these two lines is largest in the evening, between 14:00 and 22:00 hours. This makes **A** correct. Eliminate **B**, **C**, and **D** because the gaps in the lines between these hours are smaller than the gap between 14:00 and 22:00 hours.

2.   **H**   Use the Chart

Table 1 shows that Type 1 sites had decreased NO_2 emissions during the road closures, as compared to non-convention traffic. Type 1 sites are located near closed-down roads with no nearby alternative routes. Type 1 sites were hypothesized to have decreased NO_2 emissions, and this hypothesis is supported by the data. The correct answer is **H**. **F** and **J** can be eliminated because the hypothesis refers only to Type 1 sites.

3.   **C**   Read the Chart

Figure 2 shows a general consistency between convention and non-convention traffic patterns for all three sites. The dotted line follows the solid line closely in all three graphs, over all hours in the day. **A**, **B**, and **D** are therefore incorrect because the differences in traffic patterns at all sites were relatively minimal throughout the day. **C** is the best choice.

4.   **G**   Use the Chart

Table 1 shows that Type 2 sites averaged 14 ppb of NO_2 during road closures, compared to 12 ppb for non-convention traffic. This reflects an increase of 2 ppb during the convention. The increase experienced by Type 2 sites supports the hypothesis. **F** is incorrect because Type 3 sites experienced an NO_2 *decrease* of 1 ppb. The correct answer is **G**.

5.   **D**   Use the Chart

Table 1 shows that Type 1 sites had reduced NO_2 emissions during the road closures. If lower traffic volumes lead to reduced NO_2, then Type 1 sites should be the highways with the greatest reduction in traffic during the convention. I-93 South in Figure 1 had the largest reduction of traffic during the convention, so it's most likely of all the choices to be a Type I site. **D** is therefore correct. Eliminate **A**, **B**, and **C** because these routes did not have as much of a *reduction* in traffic during the convention. These routes probably did not see a change in NO_2 levels during the convention, since their traffic volumes did not decrease.

PRACTICE SET 4: RESEARCH SUMMARIES

Passage IV

Citation: Cheyne SM (2006) Wildlife reintroduction: considerations of habitat quality at the release site. *BMC Ecology* 6(5): e273. DOI: **10.1186/1472-6785-6-5**

Gibbons are small apes that live in trees. A pair of adult gibbons was raised in captivity and released on Mintin Island in Indonesia. A research scientist conducted several studies to determine whether Mintin Island could support released gibbons without negatively impacting the island's ecology.

Study 1

A review of the literature was conducted to determine the ten most important food trees for gibbons. The results are in Table 1.

Table 1		
Family	**Genus/species**	**Productivity index**
Guttifferae	*Garcinia bancana*	3.03
Moraceae	*Ficus benjamina*	3.69
Euphorbiaceae	*Baccaurea sp*	2.67
Guttifferae	*Callophyllum hosei*	6.14
Myrtaceae	*Eugenia sp*	1.98
Annonaceae	*Polyalthia sp*	2.33
Moraceae	*Artocarpus sp*	2.91
Anacardiaceae	*Mangifera foetida*	2.80
Polygalaceae	*Xanthophyllum sp*	2.41
Dillenaceae	*Dillenia reticulata*	1.09

Study 2

A comparative study was conducted of other gibbon sites to determine the relationship between trees and gibbon density in those locations. The study compared four different sites to determine what percentage of the trees on each site were one of the ten most important gibbon food trees. The study also determined the number of dipterocarp trees per hectare at each site. Dipterocarps are not common food sources for gibbons, but they are used for sleeping and singing. The results of the study are in Table 2.

Table 2				
Site	**% of trees on important species list**	**Gibbons/km²**	**% Dipterocarps**	**Gibbons/km²**
Sepilok	9.4	5.5	Not available	Not available
Kuala Lompat	10.3	6 (or 8.4)	1.0	6.0 (or 8.4)
Pasoh	12.1	8.4	Not available	Not available
Barito Ulu	18.3	10.5	42.6	18.3

Study 3

Figs are an important food source for gibbons because of their asynchronous fruiting pattern. Fig tree fruiting patterns are called *asynchronous* because all trees do not fruit at the same time. The asynchronous pattern ensures that there are always some fig trees in fruit in the forest. This makes figs an important fall-back food for gibbons in times of food shortage. A comparative study was conducted of other gibbon sites to determine the relationship between fig density and the size of the gibbon population. The results are in Table 3.

Table 3			
Site	Figs/hectare	Group Size	Groups/km²
Sepilok, Sabah	0	1.5	2.7
Tanjung Puting, Kalimantan	1.0	2.9	3.0
Siberut, Mentawai Islands	1.3	2.1	3.7
Sungai Sakam, West Malaysia	2.0	2.5	3.3
Danum, Sabah	2.3	2.1	3.5
Pasoh, West Malaysia	4.0	2.1	4.0
Barito Ulu, Kalimantan	6.0	3.6	2.8
Kutai, East Kalimantan	6.6	3.6	4.0
Kuala Lompat, West Malaysia	8.0	4.1	4.0
Ketambe, North Sumatra	27.0	4.3	4.5

1. According to the information in Study 3, the number of gibbons per square kilometer in Pasoh, West Malaysia, is:

    A. 2.1.
    B. 2.8.
    C. 4.0.
    D. 8.4.

2. Which of the following figures best represents the relationship between the percentage of trees on the important species list and the number of gibbons per square kilometer?

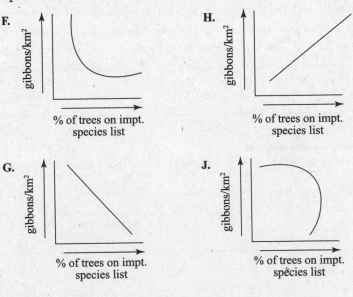

F.

H.

G.

J.

3. Mintin Island has 1.8% dipterocarp trees. Based on the results of Study 2, which of the following is likely to be the population density of gibbons on Mintin Island?
   A. 5.7 gibbons/km²
   B. 12 gibbons/km²
   C. 18.4 gibbons/km²
   D. 42.6 gibbons/km²

4. According to Study 3, which of the following statements best describes the relationship, if any, between the number of figs per hectare and gibbon group size?
   F. As the number of figs per hectare increases, gibbon group size increases.
   G. As the number of figs per hectare increases, gibbon group size stays the same.
   H. As the number of figs per hectare increases, gibbon group size decreases.
   J. There is no clear relationship between the number of figs per hectare and gibbon group size.

5. If 17% of the trees on Mintin Island are on the ten most important gibbon food tree list, according to Study 2, the number of gibbons/km² would most likely be:
   A. fewer than 5.5.
   B. between 6 and 8.4.
   C. between 8.4 and 10.5.
   D. more than 10.5.

6. What would be the best way to study which of the ten most important trees has the greatest impact on gibbon population density?
   F. Counting the percentage of each tree type and the numbers of gibbons per square kilometer for multiple locations
   G. Counting the number of gibbons living in locations with the most highly productive trees
   H. Counting the number of gibbons living in locations with the least productive trees
   J. Counting the number of gibbons that survive in locations that have relatively few fig trees per hectare

PRACTICE SET 4: ANSWERS & EXPLANATIONS

1. **D** Use the Chart
Table 3 lists the group size for each location and the number of groups per square kilometer. Group size refers to the number of individual gibbons in each group at that location. To find the number of gibbons per square kilometer, you must multiply the group size by the number of groups. For Pasoh, West Malaysia, each group contains 2.1 gibbons, and there are 4.0 groups/km². Multiply group size by the number of groups: 2.1 × 4.0 = 8.4. The correct answer is **D**.

2. **H** Handle Graphs
Table 2 lists the percentage of trees on the important species list and the number of gibbons per square kilometer at four different sites. As the percentage of trees

on the important species list increases, the number of gibbons per square kilometer increases. This relationship is represented by a straight line slanting upward to the right. This makes **H** correct. **G** is incorrect because it reflects that gibbons increase as the percentage of trees decreases. This is the *opposite* of the information given in Table 2.

3. **B** Use the Chart
    Study 2 contains two data points to show the relationship between dipterocarp trees and gibbon population. These data points suggest that the number of gibbons increases as the percentage of dipterocarps increases. If the percentage of dipterocarps on Mintin Island is 1.8, this percentage falls between that of Kuala Lompat (1.0%) and Barito Ulu (42.6%). The number of gibbons/km^2 should also fall between 6.0 and 18.3. The correct answer is **B**. The number 5.7, **A**, would be too low, and **C** and **D** would be too high.

4. **J** Use the Chart
    Study 3 shows that as the number of figs per hectare increases, gibbon group size sometimes increases and sometimes decreases. Therefore, **J** is correct. **F** is incorrect because gibbon group size does not continually increase. At 1.0 figs per hectare, for instance, group size is 2.9. At 1.3 figs per hectare, group size goes down to 2.1.

5. **C** Use the Chart
    Table 2 shows that the number of gibbons/km^2 increases as the percentage of trees on the important species list increases. If 17% of Mintin Island's trees are on the important species list, then Mintin Island falls between Pasoh (12.1%) and Barito Ulu (18.3%). Pasoh has 8.4 gibbons/km^2, and Barito Ulu has 10.5. Mintin Island is most likely to have a number between 8.4 and 10.5. The correct answer is **C**. The numbers given in **A** and **B** are too low, and **D** is wrong because it is too high.

6. **F** Take the Next Step
    This methodology question asks you for the best way to determine which tree has the greatest impact on gibbon populations. A comparative study that assessed other locations would be helpful. The study could identify the ten most important tree types by percentage for each location. It could also count the number of gibbons/km^2. Patterns in the data for all sites would help pinpoint which trees are present with the largest populations of gibbons. **F** is therefore the correct answer. Eliminate **G** and **H** because the study aims to compare the impact of all ten different types of trees, not the impact of the most or least productive trees. **J** is also incorrect because the study does not concern fig trees in particular.

PRACTICE SET 5: RESEARCH SUMMARIES

Passage V

Citation: Komatsu F., Kagawa Y., Sakuma M., Kawabata T., Kaneko Y., et al. (2006) Investigation of oxidative stress and dietary habits in Mongolian people, compared to Japanese people. *Nutrition & Metabolism* 3(21): e273. DOI: **10.1186/1743-7075-3-21**

The average life span of Mongolians is 62 years for males and 69 years for females. This life span is considerably shorter than that of Japanese men and women, who live for 79 and 85 years, respectively. Mongolians generally eat meat, fat, and dairy products, consuming fewer vegetables or fruit than do the Japanese. A group of scientists conducted studies on both groups to determine the relationship between dietary habits and longevity.

Study 1

Researchers conducted interviews to determine the daily food intake of Mongolian and Japanese subjects. The interviews were conducted using a Food Frequency Questionnaire developed at Kagawa Nutrition University. The results are in Table 1.

Table 1		
Food (average grams/day)	**Mongolian Subjects (average grams/day)**	**Japanese Subjects (average grams/day)**
Rice	68.1	369.4
Flour Products	264.1	102.9
Potatoes	59.1	57.6
Vegetables	72.2	286.4
Eggs	4.3	37.3
Meat	122.7	84.3
Fish	5.5	90.9
Dairy Products	430.1	95.7
Fruits	29.5	101.4
Fat	31.1	11.2
Sweets	14.7	23.9
Seasoning	23.6	103.7
Tea, Soft Drinks & Alcohol	957.2	684.3

Study 2

One marker for longevity is levels of oxidative stress. Oxidative stress occurs when the body overproduces compounds called *reactive oxygen species* (ROS). Oxidative stress leads to cell damage, which has been shown to be correlated with early aging and shortened life spans. Oxidative stress was measured by testing the levels of reactive oxygen metabolites (ROM) in Mongolian and Japanese subjects. ROM levels were expressed in units known as Carr U. The results are in Figure 1. Each dot represents a measurement for one individual. ROM levels averaged 429.7 Carr U for Mongolian subjects and 335.3 Carr U for Japanese subjects.

The ACT Math & Science Workbook

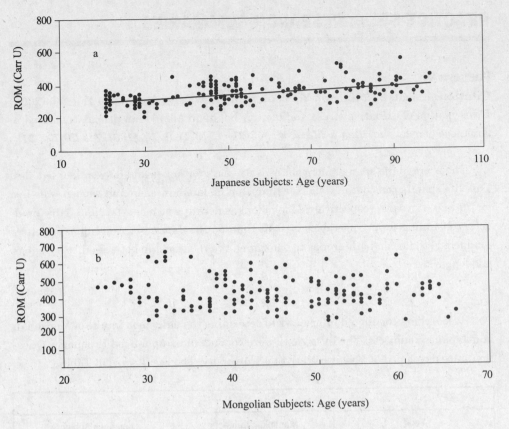

Figure 1

1. According to the information in Study 2, which of the following statements best describes the relationship between age and ROM levels in Mongolian subjects?
   A. As age increases, ROM levels increase.
   B. As age increases, ROM levels decrease.
   C. As age increases, ROM levels first increase and then decrease.
   D. There is no clear relationship between age and ROM levels.

2. According to the information in Study 1, Mongolian and Japanese subjects differ most in their average daily food intake in grams for which food category?
   F. Rice
   G. Dairy Products
   H. Tea, Soft Drinks, and Alcohol
   J. Flour Products

3. Which of the following conclusions is most strongly supported by the information in Study 1?
   A. Mongolians do not like eggs as much as the Japanese do.
   B. Mongolians eat more fish and less meat, on average, than do the Japanese.
   C. In Japan, a serving of potatoes costs about six times as much as a serving of rice.
   D. The Japanese eat less fat per day, on average, than do Mongolians.

4. What would be the best way to study the effects of fruit and vegetable intake on oxidative stress?

   F. Varying the amount of fruit and vegetables that both groups consume while eliminating soft drinks and sugar

   G. Varying the amount of fruit that both groups consume while keeping the vegetable intake constant

   H. Varying the amount of fruit and vegetables that both groups consume while keeping the remaining food intake constant

   J. Varying the amount of other food that both groups consume while keeping fruit and vegetable intake constant

5. Intake of fruits and vegetables is hypothesized to reduce oxidative stress because fruits and vegetables contain compounds that fight oxidation in the body. Do the results of Studies 1 and 2 support this hypothesis?

   A. Yes, because Japanese subjects consumed more fruits and vegetables and had lower average ROM levels than did Mongolian subjects.

   B. No, because Japanese subjects consumed more fruits and vegetables and had higher average ROM levels than did Mongolian subjects.

   C. Yes, because Mongolian subjects consumed more fruits and vegetables and had lower average ROM levels than did Japanese subjects.

   D. No, because Mongolian subjects consumed more fruits and vegetables and had higher average ROM levels than did Japanese subjects.

6. Scientists measure the ROM level of a 68-year-old Japanese subject who eats a diet similar to that of the other Japanese subjects. Based on the information in Figure 2, the new subject will most likely have a ROM level closest to:

   F. 200 Carr U.

   G. 400 Carr U.

   H. 700 Carr U.

   J. The ROM level cannot be determined from the information given.

PRACTICE SET 5: ANSWERS & EXPLANATIONS

1. **D** Handle Graphs

   The passage states that each dot in Figure 1 represents a measurement for one individual. If the dots are clustered in a particular trend, then a relationship is indicated. **A** is incorrect because this relationship applies to the Japanese subjects only. The line slanting upward on the graph shows that as age increases for Japanese subjects, ROM levels also tend to increase. In the Mongolian graph, however, the dots are distributed randomly. Some young subjects have high ROM levels, while some older subjects have low ROM levels. Most of the subjects have readings somewhere in the middle of the graph, with no clear patterns. So, there does not appear to be a relationship between age and ROM in these subjects. The correct answer is **D**.

2.   **G**   Use the Chart

According to Table 1, Mongolian subjects consumed 430.1 grams of dairy products per day on average. Japanese subjects, by contrast, consumed an average of only 95.7 grams per day. Mongolians consumed 334.4 grams more dairy products per day than did the Japanese. This difference is the largest reflected in the table. **F** reflects a difference of 301.3 grams, while **H** reflects a difference of 272.9 grams. So, **G** is correct.

3.   **D**   Read the Chart

Table 1 reveals that Japanese subjects consumed an average of 11.2 grams of fat per day. Mongolian subjects consumed an average of 31.1 grams per day. From these figures, we can conclude that the Japanese eat less fat per day, on average, than do Mongolians. The study revealed nothing about food costs, so **C** is incorrect. It's also too much of a leap to conclude that either group *likes* certain foods more. From the table, it can be concluded that they *consume* these foods more. There could be many reasons—including scarcity—why a group doesn't eat certain foods. So, **A** can be eliminated. The best choice is **D**.

4.   **H**   Take the Next Step

To determine the impact of one factor on another, you must change the first factor while keeping other factors constant. This approach helps to ensure that your results are only influenced by the one factor that you've changed. In this case, to study how fruits and vegetables affect oxidative stress, you would vary the amounts of fruits and vegetables that subjects consume while keeping other food intake constant. Eliminate **F** and **G** because *all* other food intake would need to be held constant. The correct answer is **H**.

5.   **A**   Use the Chart

Table 1 shows that Japanese subjects consumed more fruit and vegetables per day, on average, than did Mongolian subjects. So, **C** and **D** are incorrect. Figure 1 and the passage indicate that Japanese subjects had lower ROM levels overall as well. Increased fruit and vegetable consumption is associated here with lower ROM levels, which supports the hypothesis in question. The correct answer is **A**.

6.   **G**   Use the Chart

Figure 2 shows that the ROM levels of Japanese subjects cluster around a central line. Near age 70, ROM readings cluster around 400 Carr U. The new subject will most likely have a ROM reading closest to 400 Carr U. **F**, 200, is too low, and **H**, 700, is too high. Therefore, the correct answer is **G**.

PRACTICE SET 6: RESEARCH SUMMARIES

Passage VI

Citation: Salomon JA, Lloyd-Smith JO, Getz WM, Resch S, Sánchez MS, et al. (2006) Prospects for advancing tuberculosis control efforts through novel therapies. PLoS Med 3(8): e273. DOI: *10.1371/journal.pmed.0030273*

The current treatment for tuberculosis (TB) extends over a six-month time period. Faster-acting medications have recently been developed that have the potential to shorten the TB treatment period. Shorter treatments may help to enhance the detection of TB as well because they are likely to encourage more individuals to start treatment. Scientists studied TB treatments to understand the likely relationships between length of treatment, detection methods, and the overall impact of tuberculosis.

Study 1

Scientists used a TB evaluation model to assess how shorter TB treatments would affect the expected duration of TB cases. The results are in Figure 1. The default rate, shown on the horizontal axis, reflects the percentage of individuals who discontinue treatment. The solid black line represents treatment durations of six months. The solid gray line represents treatment durations of four months. The dotted line represents treatment durations of two months.

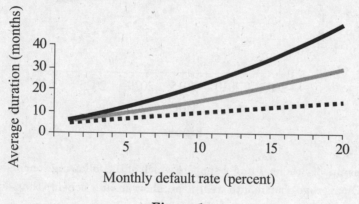

Figure 1

Study 2

The evaluation model was used to assess how treatment length would affect the expected number of secondary TB cases. Secondary TB cases are those that are generated by an average original case. Secondary TB cases are one measure of how extensively TB spreads within a population. The results are in Figure 2. The solid black line represents treatment durations of 6 months. The solid gray line represents treatment durations of four months. The dotted line represents treatment durations of two months.

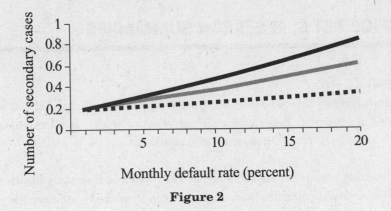

Figure 2

Study 3

Scientists used a mathematical model to project the number of new cases of TB for a particular geographic region. The results are in Figure 3. The solid black line represents projections with current TB treatments. The solid gray line represents projections with shorter treatments (four months and two months combined). The dotted line represents projections with enhanced methods of detecting TB.

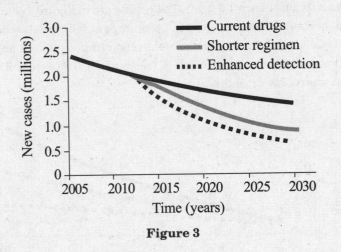

Figure 3

1. The results of Studies 1 and 2 support which of the following conclusions?
   A. On average, four-month treatments show greater benefits than do two-month treatments.
   B. Shorter treatments are helpful for reducing the duration of TB but not the number of secondary cases.
   C. The benefits of shorter treatments increase as the percentage default rate increases.
   D. The outcomes of six-month treatments remain fairly consistent regardless of the percentage default rate.

2. If Study 1 were repeated, this time examining the results under 25% default rates, which of the following would be the expected duration of TB with a six-month treatment?
   F. 10 months
   G. 20 months
   H. 40 months
   J. 50 months

3. In Study 3, after 2010, new cases are projected to be reduced further by en-hanced detection than they are by shorter treatments. Which of the following statements is the most likely explanation for the additional reduction in new cases?

   A. Current medications are not successful in treating some individuals, mak-ing it more likely that they will relapse.

   B. Enhanced detection brings patients into treatment earlier, shortening the time they have to transmit TB to others.

   C. Shorter treatment regimes make individuals more likely to stick with their treatments instead of dropping out.

   D. Enhanced detection methods are usually carried out only after traditional detection methods are complete.

4. According to the results of Study 3, in 2005, current drug treatments resulted in how many new cases of TB?

   F. 1.0 million

   G. 1.5 million

   H. 2.5 million

   J. 4.0 million

5. To further investigate the effect of shorter treatment on the impact of TB, the scientists should repeat Study:

   A. 1, examining the cure rate of each treatment type.

   B. 1, examining who might invent the shorter treatments.

   C. 2, examining the cost of shorter treatments.

   D. 3, examining the number of current drugs used.

6. According to the results of Study 2, under what conditions is the number of sec-ondary cases lowest?

   F. Six-month treatment with a 10% default rate

   G. Four-month treatment with a 20% default rate

   H. Six-month treatment with a 15% default rate

   J. Four-month treatment with an 18% default rate

PRACTICE SET 6: ANSWERS & EXPLANATIONS

1. **C** Use the Chart

   A is incorrect because on both graphs two-month treatment regimens produce the best results. **B** is incorrect for the same reason. Two-month treatment regimens produce the greatest reduction in duration of TB as well as secondary cases. Fig-ures 1 and 2 show that as the percentage default rate increases, shorter treat-ments produce more gains, compared against longer treatments. For instance, Figure 1 shows that when 5% of patients drop out of treatment, the two-month treatment plan reduces the duration of TB from 10 months to about 5 months. When 20% of patients drop out, however, the two-month plan reduces TB duration from 40 months to 10 months. The same types of benefits ensue for the reduction of secondary cases, shown in Figure 2. So, **C** is correct.

2. **J** Use the Chart

The graph in Figure 1 shows that average case duration increases steadily as the default rate percentage increases. This is true for all three lengths of treatment. At a 25% default rate, the case duration with a 6-month treatment is likely to be *greater* than 40 months. **F, G,** and **H** are all too small, considering the trend shown by the graph. This makes **J** the best choice.

3. **B** Use the Chart

If enhanced detection brings patients into treatment earlier, this means that patients have less time to transmit TB to others. Fewer transmissions will likely result in fewer new cases. **B** is therefore the correct answer. **A** is incorrect because it explains the higher numbers of new cases under current treatments—not the reason for even fewer new cases with enhanced detection. **C** is also incorrect because it explains the results of shorter treatment regimens, not enhanced detection.

4. **H** Read the Chart

The black line in Figure 3 indicates the number of new cases seen over time with current drug treatments. In 2005, the number of new cases was 2.5 million. So, **H** is correct.

5. **A** Take the Next Step

In Study 1, scientists investigate how well shorter treatments help to reduce the *duration* of TB. Another helpful study would be to asses how well shorter treatments help to *cure* TB, compared to longer treatments. The scientists could repeat Study 1, this time looking at cure rates. This makes **A** correct. **B** and **C** are wrong because looking at inventors and costs would not help scientists understand the effect of the shorter treatments on TB. Eliminate **D** because it looks at current treatments, not shorter ones.

6. **F** Read the Chart

Figure 2 shows all three lines slanted upward to the right. On any line, the number of secondary cases gets lower as you move toward the left of the graph. **F** reflects about 0.4 secondary cases, the fewest of all the answer choices. **G** reflects nearly 0.6 secondary cases, **H** reflects 0.6, and **J** reflects approximately 0.5. So, eliminate **G, H,** and **J**. The correct answer is **F**.

PRACTICE SET 7: CONFLICTING VIEWPOINTS

Passage VII

The Sahel region is a semi-arid zone located south of the Sahara Desert in Africa. In the mid to late 1900s, the region suffered from extended drought. Today, scientists disagree about how environmental conditions will affect future rainfall in Sahel. Two hypotheses are discussed.

Wet Sahel Hypothesis

The Sahel region will receive much-needed rainfall during the twenty-first century. Based on the most recent computerized climate models, greenhouse gas emissions are predicted to cause increased precipitation in the area. Greenhouse gas emissions are responsible for temperature changes in the Indian and Atlantic oceans. Warming of the Indian Ocean is expected to produce continued drought in portions of Africa south of the Sahel. However, temperature differentials in the Atlantic will have the opposite effect on the Sahel itself. Over the next several decades, the north Atlantic is expected to remain warmer than the south Atlantic. This temperature differential will help to redirect monsoon winds toward the Sahel, increasing precipitation there.

Dry Sahel Hypothesis

A highly accurate computer model of twentieth-century climate patterns predicts that the Sahel region is likely to experience continued drought in the twenty-first century. Some models predict that sea surface temperatures (SSTs) in the northern Atlantic ocean will warm more quickly than SSTs in the southern Atlantic, producing heavier rains over the Sahel. While the southern Atlantic is in fact expected to warm less quickly than the north, ocean temperatures will also be affected by aerosol loading, which contributes to cooling in the northern hemisphere. A second overriding factor concerns the uniform warming of ocean temperatures as a result of greenhouse gases. SSTs will be affected by uniform warming as greenhouse gases continue to warm the planet as a whole. The overall warming of SST levels is expected to be stronger than the effect of the differences in temperature, resulting in increased dryness in the Sahel despite different SST gradients.

1. The Dry Sahel Hypothesis would be most strengthened by finding that SSTs in the south Atlantic ocean:
   A. demonstrate a pattern of increased warming each year.
   B. show resistance to the warming effects of greenhouse gases.
   C. remain stable despite documented aerosol loading.
   D. warm more quickly than SSTs in the northern Atlantic.

2. Based on the information in both hypotheses, scientific predictions of climate outcomes can be best developed through studying:
   F. the economic effects of long-term drought.
   G. ways to reduce greenhouse emissions.
   H. the impact of ocean temperatures on rainfall.
   J. differences in pathways of aerosol loading.

3. The scientists supporting both hypotheses would agree that SSTs in the Atlantic Ocean are likely to:

    A. warm less quickly than SSTs in the Indian ocean.

    B. affect levels of precipitation in the Sahel region.

    C. be unaffected by levels of aerosol loading.

    D. help direct monsoon winds away from the Sahel.

4. The Wet Sahel Hypothesis predicts that over the next several decades, the north Atlantic will:

    F. have warmer temperatures than the south Atlantic.

    G. warm at a slower rate than the south Atlantic.

    H. experience more monsoons than the Indian Ocean.

    J. experience more drastic temperature changes.

5. If it was discovered that monsoon winds had increased near the Sahel, how would this discovery affect the hypotheses, if at all?

    A. It would have no effect on either hypothesis.

    B. It is consistent with the Dry Sahel Hypothesis only.

    C. It is consistent with both hypotheses.

    D. It is consistent with the Wet Sahel Hypothesis only.

6. Based on the information in both hypotheses, greenhouse gases lead to:

    F. relief from widespread drought.

    G. ocean temperature changes.

    H. cooling in the northern hemisphere.

    J. erratic climate patterns.

7. Uniform warming due to greenhouse emissions is predicted by:

    A. the Wet Sahel Hypothesis only.

    B. both of the hypotheses.

    C. neither of the hypotheses.

    D. the Dry Sahel Hypothesis only.

PRACTICE SET 7: ANSWERS & EXPLANATIONS

1.   **A** Inference

The Dry Sahel Hypothesis claims that greenhouse gases will make both north and south Atlantic temperatures warmer overall. This overall warming is predicted to cause drying of the Sahel, even if the south Atlantic warms less quickly than the north Atlantic. The Dry Sahel Hypothesis would be supported if scientists could show that south Atlantic SSTs are becoming warmer overall each year. So, **A** is correct. **B** is incorrect because it is the opposite of information given in the text. According to paragraph 3, SSTs should be affected by greenhouse gases.

2.   **H**   Comparison
Both hypotheses discuss how ocean temperatures affect climate outcomes. Specifically, they explain how differences in temperatures affect rainfall. The correct answer is **H**. Neither passage discusses **F**, the effects of long-term drought. Aerosol loading is only discussed by the Dry Sahel Hypothesis, so eliminate **J**.

3.   **B**   Comparison
Paragraph 2 states that temperatures in the Atlantic Ocean will cause increased rain in the Sahel. Paragraph 3 states that Atlantic Ocean temperatures will cause dryness in the Sahel. This makes **B** correct. Neither passage compares the warming rates of the Atlantic Ocean with those of the Indian Ocean, so **A** can be ruled out. **C** is wrong because aerosol loading is discussed only in paragraph 3. **D** is wrong because monsoon winds are discussed only in paragraph 2.

4.   **F**   Detail
The sixth sentence of paragraph 2 states that *the north Atlantic is expected to remain warmer than the south Atlantic*. The correct answer is **F**.

5.   **D**   Inference
Paragraph 2 predicts that differences in Atlantic Ocean temperatures are likely to redirect monsoon winds over the Sahel, causing rainfall in the Sahel. If more monsoon winds were found near the Sahel, this would support the Wet Sahel Hypothesis. The Dry Sahel Hypothesis does not predict increased monsoon winds over the Sahel, so **B** and **C** can be eliminated. The best choice is **D**.

6.   **G**   Comparison
Both hypotheses state that greenhouse gases cause changes in ocean temperature. However, they disagree over the nature of those changes. The Wet Sahel Hypothesis argues that greenhouse gases will increase rainfall, while the Dry Sahel Hypothesis argues the opposite. Greenhouse gases are seen by both hypotheses as causing predictable climate patterns rather than erratic ones, so eliminate **J**. The correct answer is **G**.

7.   **D**   Detail
The third paragraph states that *SSTs will be affected by uniform warming as greenhouse gases continue to warm the planet as a whole*. The second paragraph doesn't mention uniform warming, so **A** and **B** can be eliminated. The correct answer is **D**.

PRACTICE SET 8: CONFLICTING VIEWPOINTS

Passage VIII

A scientific theory of how our solar system originated must meet several requirements. Explaining how the planets formed with solid cores is only one requirement. The theory must also explain other phenomena, such as why the sun is at the center of the solar system and why the planets lie at predictable distances from the sun. Accomplishing these requirements is a formidable task. Two theories are presented.

Nebular Theory

The solar system was formed from a cloud of gas and dust known as the solar nebula. The solar nebula consisted of slowly rotating matter with two to three times the mass of the sun. Over time, it collapsed inward on itself and began to rotate more quickly. The rapid rotation shaped the nebula into a flattened, disk-shaped cloud with gaseous rings surrounding its contracted center. The gaseous rings surrounding the center of the nebula spun off into great bodies of matter, which contracted to become the planets. The nebula's center continued to condense until eventually the process of thermonuclear fusion began and the sun was formed.

High Mass Star Theory

The solar system originated as the result of energy shock waves from a very high mass star. The high mass star had a short, explosive life, releasing large amounts of energy and bombarding its nearby environment with intense ultraviolet radiation. This radiation formed a region that expanded into space, producing a low-mass sun surrounded by a disk of pre-planetary matter. As radiation continued to bombard the low-mass sun, the pre-planetary matter formed into planets. The high mass star then exploded in an event known as a supernova, showering the solar system with isotopes such as iron-60.

1. The High Mass Star Theory does NOT discuss which of the following?
   A. Ultraviolet radiation
   B. Iron-60
   C. Thermonuclear fusion
   D. A supernova explosion

2. Which of the following is discussed in the passage by the High Mass Star Theory, but NOT by the Nebular Theory?
   F. The release of energy shock waves
   G. The origin of the solar system
   H. The formation of the planets
   J. Condensation of the solar nebula

3. Supporters of both theories would agree with the conclusion that:
   A. the solar system was created by the explosion of a supernova.
   B. the formation of the sun occurred long before that of the planets.
   C. the planets were created from gaseous rings that spun into matter.
   D. the formation of the sun is linked with the formation of the planets.

4. Which of the following, if discovered by scientists, would provide the most support for the High Mass Star Theory?
   F.   Solar nebulas that rotate at rapid speeds around an axis
   G.   Isotopes of iron-60 in meteorites in our solar system
   H.   High-mass star explosions in distant solar systems
   J.   A low-mass sun surrounded by multiple gaseous rings

5. Assuming that the Nebular Theory is correct, which of the following conclusions can be made about the sun and the planets?
   A.   Both originated in an environment that was bombarded with radiation.
   B.   Both developed as the result of the thermonuclear fusion process.
   C.   In their early stages, they both went through a contraction process.
   D.   A high-mass sun is ultimately responsible for the appearance of both.

6. Which of the following is mentioned by the High Mass Star Theory, but is NOT developed in the passage?
   F.   High-mass star radiation
   G.   Gravitational tides
   H.   Solar nebula rotation
   J.   Supernova explosions

7. Proponents of the two theories disagree over whether the planets formed due to:
   A.   supernova explosions or meteorite collisions.
   B.   rapid rotation or bombardment by radiation.
   C.   high-mass star activity or low-mass star activity.
   D.   radioactive isotopes or thermonuclear fusion.

PRACTICE SET 8: ANSWERS & EXPLANATIONS

1.   **C** Detail
     A, **B**, and **D** are all mentioned in the High Mass Star Theory. However, thermonuclear fusion is not mentioned in the paragraph regarding the High Mass Star Theory. Thermonuclear fusion is only mentioned in the paragraph on the Nebular Theory, so **C** is correct.

2.   **F** Comparison
     The release of energy shock waves is mentioned in the first sentence of paragraph 3 but is not mentioned elsewhere in the passage. Both theories discuss the origins of the solar system, **G**, and the formation of the planets, **H**. Only the Nebular Theory discusses **J**, the condensation of the solar nebula. This makes **F** correct.

3.   **D** Comparison
     The Nebular Theory explains how the planets and the sun both formed out of the solar nebula. The High Mass Star Theory explains how the planets and the sun both formed as a result of radiation from a high mass star. Therefore, both theories describe the formation of the planets and the sun as linked. The Nebular

Theory describes the sun as forming *after* the planets were formed, so **B** is incorrect. The correct answer is **D**.

4. **G**   Inference
    The High Mass Star Theory hypothesizes that the solar system was formed by a star that eventually exploded, leaving fragments such as iron-60 isotopes in the solar system. The discovery of iron-60 isotopes in meteorites would support this view. High mass star explosions in distant solar systems would not support the theory for how *our* solar system formed, so **H** is incorrect. Solar nebulas and gaseous rings pertain to the Nebular Theory only, so **F** and **J** are out. **G** is the best choice.

5. **C**   Inference
    A and **D** both pertain only to the High Mass Star Theory, so they can be eliminated. In paragraph 2, thermonuclear fusion is described as forming only the sun, not the planets. So, **B** is wrong. The Nebular Theory does state that the sun formed out of the contracted center of a solar nebula, and the planets formed from gaseous rings that spun off and then contracted. It can be concluded from this theory, then, that both the planets and the sun went through contraction processes. Therefore, **C** is correct.

6. **J**   Detail
    High-mass star radiation is discussed throughout the third paragraph, so eliminate **F**. **G** is also incorrect because gravitational tides are never mentioned. Solar nebula rotation is discussed only in paragraph 2, so **H** is incorrect. The paragraph on the High Mass Star Theory mentions supernova explosions in the last sentence. However, supernovas are not developed in detail. So, the correct answer is **J**.

7. **B**   Comparison
    The Nebular Theory attributes planetary formation to the *rapid rotation* of a solar nebula. The High Mass Star Theory argues that planets formed when *radiation bombarded* the pre-planetary matter surrounding a low mass sun. Meteorite collisions are not discussed by either theory, so eliminate **A**. The Nebular Theory never mentions high mass or low mass stars, so **C** is wrong. **D** is also incorrect because isotopes are never discussed as *causing* planetary formation. This makes **B** correct.